Cartoons and Extremism

To Emmanuelle,
Greta and Daniel,
What would I be without you?

To Doubi
To Corinne Evens and her wonderful Foundation

congrès juif
européen

**european
jewish congress**

Cartoons and Extremism

Israel and the Jews in Arab and Western Media

Joël Kotek
Translated from the French by Alisa Jaffa

First published in 2009 by Vallentine Mitchell

Suite 314, Premier House,
112–114 Station Road,
Edgware, Middlesex
HA8 7BJ, UK

920 NE 58th Avenue, Suite 300
Portland, Oregon,
97213-3786
USA

www.vmbooks.com

Copyright © 2008 Joël Kotek

This book is published with the support and assistance of the *Anti Defamation League*, the *Community Security Trust* and the *European Jewish Congress*.

British Library Cataloguing in Publication Data

Kotek, Joël
Cartoon and extremism : Israel and the Jews in Arab and
Western media
1. Antisemitism in the press 2. Antisemitism in art 3. Jews
in art 4. Antisemitism - Caricatures and cartoons 5. Jews -
Caricatures and cartoons
I. Title
305.8'924'0207

ISBN 978 0 85303 752 1 (paper)

Library of Congress Cataloging-in-Publication Data:
A catalog record has been applied for

Printed by SNP Leefung, China

Contents

Contents

Preface

The European Jewish Congress is honoured to present this far-reaching and detailed study on the worrying proliferation of anti-Semitic cartoons in the beginning of the 21st century. In newspapers, magazines, internet sites and other forms of mass media throughout the Arab-Muslim world and beyond, filthy anti-Semitic depictions of Jews and Israel are rife. As this study shows, it risks to pollute younger generations with hate and misunderstanding.

This book is a vital contribution to the struggle against anti-Semitism and prejudice, in that it provides an informative historical analysis, in addition to displaying the harsh reality of the cartoons. The author creates a continuity between these hateful cartoons found in the contemporary mass media with the medieval European anti-Semitism that culminated in the Holocaust. And although this phenomenon is to be found mainly in the media in the "Arab-Muslim" world, this study also shows that it is also found in both the mainstream and extremist media in the West.

Since the outbreak of the Second Intifada in 2000, the European Jewish Congress has actively monitored and worked to combat the so-called "new anti-Semitism" that has characterized much of the violence against Jews in Europe. This manifestation of one of the most ancient forms of hatred comes in various forms, often hiding anti-Semitism and theories of a Jewish conspiracy behind "legitimate" criticism of Israel.

Yet as this study shows, this "new anti-Semitism" is quite old, an has is deeply rooted in ancient European Jew-hatred.

The images contained in this book - be they medieval German engravings or current newspapers read by millions - should speak for themselves.

Moshe Kantor
President, European Jewish Congress
Geneva, March 2008

Foreword

There is a nasty movement around the world called 'anti-*anti*-Semitism'. Like its first cousin 'Holocaust denial', this bigoted movement denies the reality of anti-Semitism, arguing that claims of anti-Semitism are really attacks on those who merely criticize Israel or Zionism. They deny that there is any increase in hatred directed at Jews, Judaism or the Jewish community. This book puts the lie to that movement. It is the 'smoking gun' that proves the pervasiveness of continuing, indeed increasing, anti-Semitism in many quarters. Sometimes the anti-Semitism is 'pure': it is directed only against Jews, as such. Sometimes it is mingled with anti-Zionism. But it is always filled with lies, hate, stereotyping and bigotry.

The new anti-Semitism – generated in large part by the hatred of many Arabs, Muslims, hard-left and hard-right anti-Israel extremists – mirrors the old anti-Semitism of the 1930s and 1940s. It is old, spoiled wine, in new, cracked bottles.

The new *anti*-anti-Semitism is largely a contrivance of the academic hard left. It is a totally phony movement designed to blunt legitimate criticism of those who seek to de-legitimate, demonize and isolate Israel, and to subject the Jewish state to a double standard. It seeks to limit the marketplace of ideas only to anti-Zionists, including those represented by the cartoons in this book.

The appropriate reaction to the despicable cartoons illustrated in this volume is outrage and a determination to fight bigotry. By any standards, these anti-Semitic cartoons are far worse than the Danish cartoons depicting Mohammed that started such violence around the world Yet those who peruse the cartoons in this book will not respond with violence. We should however unite in our determination to resist and repel the bigotry these cartoons represent.

Alan Dershowitz
Harvard Law School
February 2007

Foreword

Joel Kotek's study of anti-Semitic cartoons in Arab and Western cultures is a vital contribution to an understanding of the resurgence of anti-Semitism in our world today

Kotek's decision to focus on cartoons as a way to understand anti-Semitism is one we share. ADL has been monitoring anti-Semitic cartoons in the Arab world for decades and produces regular reports on the latest manifestations of this phenomenon. Cartoons both tell much about a society and can have an impact on attitudes.

This book is particularly valuable because of its comprehensive approach to the issue and because it relates current cartoons in the Arab and Muslim world to the long and pernicious history of images about Jews in the Christian world.

We learn many things from Kotek's analysis. First with all the talk about the "new anti-Semitism" reflecting the connection of anti-Semitism to anti-Zionism, the truth is there is far more about this anti-Semitism that is old rather than new.

Secondly, it reminds us how easily the centuries-old conspiracy theories about Jews that emerged in Christian societies can be adopted and adapted by very different cultures, in this case the Islamic world. It speaks to the unique character of anti-Semitism (all forms of hatred have things in common and that which makes each unique), the idea that the reality about Jews is not apparent, it is secretive, poisonous, and powerful. We see this in images of Jews as having secret ritu-als, of Jews accused of repeating the murder of Jesus, of Jews being the secret power in the world.

Thirdly, Kotek reminds us that anti-Semitism both in the Arab and Muslim world and in the West is a mainstream phenomenon, not something on the margin. These cartoons have appeared in publications that are read by the public on a regular basis. He reminds us, if we needed reminding, that anti-Semitism, more than 60 years after the Holocaust is not only still alive in the West, but has developed and stubbornly maintained a potency in the Arab and Islamic worlds.

Finally, Kotek alerts us to the two great dangers of the continuing anti-Semitism in the Arab world. First, if there is to be hope for peace between Israel and the Arab world, the hate found in these cartoons must cease and be countered by education for peace and respect.

Even worse, if such hatred continues, it can become the lynchpin for violence against the State of Israel and the Jewish people that we witnessed in Europe in the 20th century. Kotek's study should be a wake-up call for all who take seriously the words "Never Again."

Abraham H. Foxman
Anti-Defamation League
February 2007

Foreword

Antisemitism has been a self-inflicted catastrophe for the Arab world. It has fostered a kind of mental incontinence, disabling in its effects. It destroys understanding, it destroys peace and the prospect of peace. It has begun to flourish once again in the West too, where it has attached itself to the cause of Palestinian nationalism.

In the generality of the cartoons collected in this book, indignation is the presiding note – the visual equivalent of a shrill, abusive scream. A token satire is put at the service of an incontinent antisemitism. Most of these cartoonists from Muslim countries are no freer than their journalist colleagues to express their own views. They must work within prescribed perspectives; they may only attack prescribed targets. But if they are not free to choose their enemies, they compensate in the violence with which they attack those enemies allowed to them. These cartoonists are thus subversive of nothing but human decency. The independent-minded few who operate outside these constraints tend to live outside the Muslim world, and/or die unnatural deaths – consider the career of the late Naji Salim al-Ali, murdered in London in 1987. The safest topics tend also to be the ones most susceptible to dishonest treatment – and none is safer, or more dishonest, than the topic of the blood libel. In the blood libel cartoons, the cartoonists' pencils lie. These lies are especially dangerous because cartoons are hard to contest; it is difficult to argue

with them, because they themselves are not discursive. They comprise not so much an allegation as a representation of reality. They simplify, condense and intensify. They cross linguistic and national borders. The blood libel cartoons have all Jews in their sights. Their most immediate precedents are the cartoons of Philip Ruprecht ('Fips') that appeared in *Der Stürmer* from December 1925 until 1945, their somewhat earlier precedents are to be found among the woodcuts and engravings of medieval times.

The blood libel has a greater density of reference, a greater historical and ideological resonance, than the more commonplace, everyday lies that people tell. But the blood libel will always be a lie, nonetheless. It is a demonstration of that great counter-intuitive truth that sometimes there can be smoke without fire.

At the end of the eleventh century the armies of the First Crusade made their way through the Rhineland, killing, raping and plundering Jews. Entire communities were destroyed; hundreds of lives were lost, while the lives of those Jews who survived were ruined. Among the leaders of these massacring bands was one Count Emicho. He and his cohorts fell upon the city of Worms on 18 May 1096, and immediately encountered a problem. How to incite the local populace to assist them in their planned assault on the city's Jews? The Mainz Chronicle, written by a late eleventh-century Jew, tells the story:

They took a trampled corpse of theirs, which had been buried thirty days previously, and carried it through the city, saying, 'Behold what the Jews have done to our comrade. They took a gentile and boiled him in water. They then poured the water into our wells in order to kill us.'

That is to say, they just made it up. It was a *ruse de guerre*, or more accurately, a *ruse de massacre*. The lie seems to have worked; almost the entire community was killed. The lie also seems to have been a new one. The received historical wisdom is that the allegation of well-poisoning was not made until early in the fourteenth century. The lie is perhaps best regarded as a preparatory to far greater, more consequential lies. But it invites one conclusion.

What began in deceit and defamation continues to this day in deceit and defamation. It has throughout been an affair of hateful and hating accusations, false and lethal in equal measure. When Trotsky contemplated the spectacle of the Beilis blood libel trial, in all its vicious absurdity, its cruelty and its charlatanism, he was consumed by a 'feeling of physical nausea'. Who could not similarly be affected, surveying the history of this foul lie against the Jewish people? A strong stomach is needed to survey the pages that follow; the author is to be commended for the fortitude with which he has assembled the material.

Anthony Julius
London, September 2007

Author's Notes

For some observers, including us, the Conference against Racism, Racial Discrimination, Xenophobia and Intolerance, better known as the 'Durban Conference' (where it was held in South Africa in autumn 2001) represents a turning point. It is one of those moments in the history of ideologies and attitudes of mind, when humanity makes an abrupt shift from one way of thinking to another. The Durban meeting was intended to denounce and combat racism in all its most varied forms and diverse aspects… Yet curiously the accusations levelled focused on one specific population: they targeted the Jews. Strange, but not altogether surprising, and made even worse by the lack of any reaction on the part of most of the delegates in attendance from the Western NGOs. For the overwhelming majority of these, the distribution of racist images and comments in a gathering dedicated to combating racial prejudice in fact, seemed to present no problem.

What is this all about? And what does it conceal? For us these were the questions that immediately arose. In search of an answer we left Durban, where 'the scandal' erupted from a series of antisemitic cartoons distributed by an Arab organisation – and reproduced in the pages of this book. We set out on a trail that revealed hundreds and thousands of drawings of a similar nature and originating from the same geographic region. There, in the name of anti-Zionism, Jews are daily depicted as sadistic and bloodthirsty monsters, solely interested in money and power. Long linked to Western Christianity, this theme and manner of portrayal had up to now been relatively rare in the Arab-Muslim region – hence our astonishment and concern. For undoubtedly in demonising the Jew by an image worthy of Nazi propaganda publications, the intellectual elites of the Muslim world are borrowing from the worst possible exemplars. In politics, as elsewhere, hatred is the worst of mentors.

We need to make our own position clear – we have no intention of demonstrating that the Oslo Accord was a mistake. Indeed, in our view there is no doubt that Israel must put an end to the occupation of (most of) the West Bank. The withdrawal from Gaza was a blessing. It is precisely because we are in favour of a just and lasting peace between the Israelis and the Palestinians that we deemed it essential to denounce the use of hatred in the media. As well as seeking an objective approach, we want our work to be useful. One of the aims is to prove to those cartoonists, whose work we reproduce in this book, and to the editors-in-chief and to the owners of the Arab-Muslim world press, as well as to certain European journalists who have followed their example, that if they believe they are promoting the cause of peace, they are straying into dangerous territory. It does not help the Palestinian cause to portray the Israelis with whom its representatives will one day be obliged to negotiate as monsters bereft of all humanity. For there is no 'negotiation' with monsters – they have to be crushed and suppressed.

So is it our intention to contrast some kind of Jewish humanity with an alleged Arab barbarism? Are the Israelis beyond all reproach? Far from it. It goes without saying that the Palestinians could also be victims of professionals in cartoon and photomontage production. The examples in the epilogue are distressing evidence of this. For example Oleg, the Israeli cartoonist of Russian origin, working in particular for *Women in Green*, an extremist organisation advocating the support of Greater Israel, and even more unpleasant, the (American) website of *Kach*, the racist party *banned in Israel*. Banned in Israel, please note. And herein, without any doubt, lies the difference. The hate cartoons published on the two sides may appear similar, but differ in terms of their circulation. Though they appear in the majority of the major dailies in the Arab world, they have not found their way into the Israeli papers, not even the right-wing ones. In Israel the line taken by the press, even the far right, is predominantly humorous. The veteran Israeli cartoonist, Kariel Gardosh, better known as Dosh, remembers the influence once exercised by the cartoon. The press, he recalls, has always played an important role in forming Israeli public opinion. It still does, and more so than ever in the Arab world.

Hatred is the commonest element the world over, and features in all the camps involved in the Israeli–Palestinian conflict to an extent that is ever more disturbing. It is for this reason that beyond just publishing objective findings, this study is intent on raising the alarm.

Al Wafd (Egypt), 27 March 2004

Bahram Arjomandnia (Iran), 18 March 2006.
Again the myth of the Jewish hand behind the so-called Christian attacks against Islam

Cartoons, Humour and Extremism

Durban, September 2001:
The return of antisemitism

South Africa, September 2001. During a dinner organised by a group of non-governmental organisations assembled in Durban for the World Conference against Racism, Mary Robinson, United Nations High Commissioner, and one of the organisers of the *above* conference, angrily lost her normal composure. Brandishing a pamphlet distributed a moment earlier by the Union of Arab Lawyers, portraying the Jews the way only newspapers in the Hitler period could do, she burst out: *'I'm also a Jew.'* Vigorously condemning what she regarded as a profoundly antisemitic product, Mary Robinson (former President of the Irish Republic) added:

> The aim of this conference is to promote human dignity. My husband is a cartoonist; I love political cartoons, but the racism in this collection of cartoons issued by the Union of Arab Lawyers, makes me feel like saying I'm Jewish, out of solidarity with the people targeted. I know that you will find it difficult to understand me, but you are my friends, therefore I say to you I am a Jew and I will not permit such tactics to sabotage the conference. The purpose of this conference is to discuss racial discrimination, not to resolve the Israeli–Palestinian conflict.

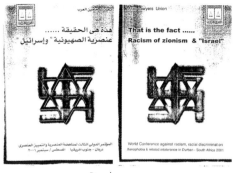

Brochure cover

Two cartoons featured in the brochure distributed by the Union of Arab Lawyers in Durban.
The Jew is shown as a Nazi, killing children.

Mary Robinson was not over-reacting by raising the spectre of antisemitism in connection with these drawings. The Union of Arab Lawyers' pamphlet was only the tip of the iceberg, revealing the distinctly unwholesome climate surrounding the conference from the very first day. Given this unhealthy climate, certain delegates chose to hide their badge of accreditation, rather than display their Israeli – or merely Jewish – origins right from the start. For in this form of international high-level assembly, it was not just a matter of getting at Israel, in the guise of conventional anti-Zionism. Here we had the militant Durban 'anti-racists' eager to thrash out the entire 'Jewish question': the Jews, all Jews (and not just Zionists or Israelis) are to blame and deserve to be indicted. Responsible for all the ills of the world. Anne Bayefsky, Professor of Law at Columbia University, New York, was under no illusions: *'I feel I'm under siege,'* she exclaimed, *'with antisemitic literature and hate all around me.'* Sizing up the situation, Yossi Sarid, leader of Israel's left-wing party, *Meretz*, endorsed the decision taken by his country's authorities by walking out of the conference, whose sole objective seemed to him to be *'from the very outset to subject Israel to a political lynching.'*

The Durban conference had already encountered some sabotage. In particular, a tract adorned with a picture of Hitler was passed around, reading as follows: *'What if he had won? There would be no Israel and no Palestinian's blood shed.'*

Undeniably, a return to anti-Jewish hatred, but of a new order since it resurfaces in line with current trends, no longer driven and distributed by the old Christian lands, the traditional world purveyors of antisemitism, but by Arab-Muslim countries.

'Anti-Zionist' poster distributed at the Durban conference. How does one characterise this poster distributed in 20,000 copies during the World Conference against Racism by South African Yousuf Deedat, who described publicly his family's connections with Osama bin Laden? Yusuf Deedat is the son of the influential Islamic 'guru' and founder of the Durban-based Islamic *Propagation Center International* (IPCI), Sheik Ahmed Deedat.

Antisemitism and its demonology: traditionally Western, currently Arab

In reviving anti-Jewish pronouncements, thought by some to have gone out of fashion forever, Durban revealed a reality that most Western observers had hitherto been unaware of – an Arab-Muslim form of antisemitism unexpectedly metamorphosed from the kind of antisemitism traditionally linked with the Christian West. We are using this term antisemitism quite deliberately – as we have written above, it is the Jew as such who finds himself targeted, attacked and demonised by this version recast as anti-Zionism. The denunciation engaged in by the enemies of the State of Israel is no longer political, or even 'philosophical', but downright racist – behind the Israeli it is the Jew that is under attack and presented as the incarnation of absolute evil.

At this point there are two possible major objections. The first is that the Arabs are Semites. How can one speak of Arab antisemitism when the Arabs are Semites themselves? It needs to be said that the term 'antisemite' was coined for the sole purpose of stigmatising the Jews alone. The concept of modern antisemitism, from Wilhelm Marr who invented the word in 1873, down to Hitler, by way of Wagner, never had anything to do with the Arabs. It was only invented – and no serious historian disputes the fact – to 'normalise' the traditional hatred of Jews, to confer on it a pseudo-scientific veneer. It is used by those who seek to summarise in one single word their specific and exclusive hatred of the Jews, be they Christians, Muslims, or even Jews. Indeed, there is a long list of the sons of the Diaspora afflicted by this suicidal neurosis, first described in Theodor Lessing's work as 'Jewish self-hatred' (*der jüdische Selbsthass*), and which led a certain Otto Weininger, the Austrian theoretician of anti-Judaism (though he was Jewish himself) and anti-feminism, to commit suicide.[1] '*He was the only Jew fit to live*', Hitler said of him.[2]

The second objection: the question of Arab antisemitism hardly arises for the simple, telling reason that there is no Arab-Muslim equivalent of traditional Christian antisemitism. A valid objection, but only to some extent. The most respected specialists agree in stressing that anti-Jewish persecutions were traditionally conducted on a far more limited scale on Islamic soil than in Christian lands. However, unfortunately it has to be said that Islamic countries are now catching up on their 'backlog'. This is the thesis put forward by Bernard Lewis, the famous Islamic scholar:

> *The first incidents of anti-Semitism in the Middle East were the work of Christian minorities and were clearly of European instigation. However they made a limited impact – so that at the time of the Dreyfus Affair in France [...] the Muslims rallied more to the side of the persecuted Jew than to his Christian persecutors. Yet the poison nevertheless continued to spread, notably after 1933, when the Nazis successfully began spreading anti-Semitic hatred into the heartland of the Arab world. The Palestine conflict greatly assisted the distribution of an anti-Semitic interpretation of history. It drove many to attribute all the troubles of the Middle East to the notion of a secret Jewish conspiracy. This interpretation now prevails in the Arab public arena, particularly in the field of education, the media and even in the entertainment and show-business industry*[3]

Cartoons are in the lead.

Why Cartoons?

This work demonstrates that the cartoon is not a documentary source like any other – each example needs to be studied for itself and must be recognised as an unfinished research subject. Gone is the time when historians could disregard fixed images such as newspaper drawings, photography, painting, strip cartoons or postcards. In a world defined above all by images, the cartoon has become one of the most popular and most effective means of communication. Nowadays a cartoon by Dave Brown, Kevin 'Kal' Kallaugher or Jeff Danzinger is undeniably just as powerful in forming public opinion as a traditional editorial, if not more so.

It was Napoleon who said that a good sketch was worth more than a long discussion.

Since then we have moved on to the present where, by means of a cartoon, a situation or a person linked to a current issue can be denounced or scorned on the spot. All it needs are a few pencil lines, sometimes just the very sketchiest and just a very few words, and the point is made. To get the message across the cartoonist will stop at nothing, sometimes outrageously inflating the tiniest defect, by pushing it to extremes, he creates a metaphor of power that exploits and corrupts, turning two overgrown canines into an image of ambition. Does a particular individual occupy high rank? Is he guilty of pride? So the cartoonist will make him more so, by placing his head in the clouds, exaggerating his haughty behaviour, his indifference to everyday matters and to common mortals. Someone who seems smug and ridiculous? Let's crush him to bits…

So are cartoons cruel? Of course they are. To expose, exaggerate, exasperate is their very nature and their function. In doing so they take a stand and commit themselves. By definition they display a lack of neutrality or mildness that is their signature. The cartoonist takes on his victim in the form of a caricature, a long-standing form of attack in which he ridicules his subject by intensifying his features.

The cartoon always expresses a commitment and is often irreverent. It mocks and denounces preferably those in power and persons of note. And this takes some courage. And even more courageous than the cartoonist who taunts the powerful and the notables, are those in control over him. The fact remains that occasionally the cartoon may turn out to be unjust and dangerous – some images are tantamount to an incitement to crime.

In this respect, as noted by René Rémond in his preface to Christian Delporte's pioneering work *Propaganda Drawings*, the cartoon is a good illustration of the state of the society that produces it: '*The study of the political cartoon,*' he says, '*is of prime interest […] for the history of political life, and further for the history of ideologies and attitudes of mind, of opinion and culture […] the cartoon is an integral part of history.*'[4]

We believe along with René Rémond, and indeed Ouriel Reshef, the perceptive author of the textbook work on the image of Germany depicted in French cartoons since the defeat of 1870, that more than any other source, cartoons provide access to the underlying attitude of a society at a particular moment in its development. '*The images created in times of crisis,*' writes Reshef, '*reveal something about the personality of those who produced them, but little more than a hallucination about the subject. Just as the dream is the main pathway to gaining access to the unconscious of the dreamer, but gives us little or no information about the contents of the dream.*'

We support the thesis of Reshef whereby '*in times of crisis – war, revolution, civil war, the psychological undercurrents of thought (stereotypes, dreams, myths) work their way up to the threshold of consciousness and burst out in cartoons. Under extreme duress the quagmire of the soul is stirred up by the upheavals and convulsions caused by events. It leaves the lower depths to rise up towards the surface where it shows through, and then sinks back again once the turmoil has subsided.*'[5]

This concept of the role of cartoons in periods of historic upheaval, alongside the assumption of a certain complicity between the artist and his public forms the theoretical basis of our research.

To demonstrate this I use the three classic 'antise-myths'[6] of Christian anti-Judaism resurrected in Arab-Muslim lands: ritual murder and the desecration of the Host or

Iraq and Palestine Crucified
Jalal Al-Rifai, *Ad Dustour*, 18 March 2004

the myth of the Jewish deicide; the blood libel of the Jew drinking blood and stealing organs; and the Jewish world conspiracy or the demon Jew seeking world domination.

In support of the argument I look back to an earlier time and recall how these anti-Jewish myths were born in the West, how and why they developed and flourished there throughout the Middle Ages right up to the present time to serve as a basis and justification for the Nazi barbarism. The second chapter examines how, following the Shoah, these myths have lost all credibility in the West, only to resurface in support of the Middle East conflict in the countries of the Arab-Muslim region. And the third part considers how by a perverse and complex mechanism these myths and portrayals from another age have little by little reappeared amongst us. The last section reveals how the same subject, indeed the same drawing can serve the interests of seemingly contradictory propagandists of the Arab cause, the heralds of an alternative globalisation and the representatives of the extreme far right, in the United

States as well as on our continent.

Our study draws on a sample of the more typical drawings, taken from the Arab as well as the Western press, where in the name of anti-Zionism and denunciation of the 'existence of Israel', it is in fact all Jews that are targeted. These images are sometimes used as a vehicle for portrayals of the most virulent form of antisemitism. Outright copies or plagiarisation of images from the Nazi press, foremost *Der Stürmer*, they

Since time immemorial the Jews are supposed to be the true masters of the world. Going by the Nazi cartoon above (1943), the Jews would dominate the Soviet Union, or rather, according to the Arab cartoon (2001), the USA

resort to the usual themes (the vampire Jew, sucking the blood of nations, the Jew asserting world domination, the Jew as killer of Christ, etc.) with the same repertoire of symbols to denounce the Jewish attempt to dominate the world (children's blood, the Cross of Christ) using the same stylistic technique (the hook nosed, thick lipped, stooping Jew), and the same portrayal in animal form (the Jew depicted as the lowest species of bestial life, such as the tentacled octopus, the bat, the spider or… the pig).

It takes no genius to realise that the best way of getting rid of an individual (or a group of individuals) is by casting doubt on their humanity. Subjecting them to degradation beforehand makes it far easier then to suppress them, with the minimum of pain or remorse. Once a human being is debased to the level of a noxious creature or disgusting insect, the ground has been prepared for his physical elimination by prior justification. All the instruments of propaganda are brought into play for this undermining process, with newspaper sketches and cartoons as the weapons of choice – these go straight to the point, creating a lasting effect on the imagination, and

are frequently more effective than the most skilful form of argument. Today, as in the recent past, public opinion is swayed more by images (from cartoons to television) than by the written word.

As Marie-Anne Matard-Bonucci has reminded us, this is exactly why the cartoon emerged during the Dreyfus trial as the tool best suited for the antisemitic crusade unleashed in France at the time. It evolved in forms and to degrees hitherto unprecedented, resurfacing later in the 1930s. These images did not simply appear alongside antisemitic statements merely to illustrate them – they synthesised them, simplified them, concentrated and standardised them – 'making it easy for them to be memorized as stereotypes of human characters. This form of cartoon by its very nature led to an intensification, at least in the way it was expressed, of antisemitic discourse, and moreover contributed to the spread of prejudice across the face of Europe.[7]

In the conflict that is tearing the Middle East apart today, the cartoon emerges as an essential ingredient. The open warfare conducted on Israeli and Palestinian soil, using assault rifles, missiles, and booby-trapped cars is mirrored no less violently, though given less media coverage, by pencil strokes, Indian ink and murderous captions. In the field of propaganda it is the Israelis (and the Jews) who turn out to be the less adept and the chief victims.

The gap between the image and the word is very narrow. From Brussels to Paris, from London to Milan the Jewish community has understandably been overtaken by a gnawing sense of unease, concerned not so much by the criticisms levelled at Israel as by the very negative images weighed down with innuendo that overstep the mark in this regard. A step too far that has recently led to violent demonstrations and outbursts of hatred. European anti-Judaism, whether it comes from ill-informed North Africans, brainwashed militants on the far left, or dyed-in-the-wool fascists, has been surprisingly and unexpectedly reinforced by the hatred of Jews newly present in the Arab lands, that has bounced back in an amplified and updated form. Its output, consisting of a mixture and echo of Christian myths, medieval accusations, Nazi images, Islamist and revisionist fables, is spreading like wildfire throughout our 'global village', like a dangerous powder trail. With this book it is our intention, in all humility, to deprive it of all legitimacy. But is there still time?

Our research has focused on cartoonists in the countries bordering Israel, including the autonomous Palestinian territories. The drawings come from a variety of sources. We have drawn on the stock of cartoons patiently assembled by Esther Webman of the *Stephen Roth Institute for the Study of Racism and Antisemitism* at Tel Aviv University. Above all, we surfed the web in search of the most striking drawings, visiting dozens of sites, both Arab-Muslim and Israeli ones, or simply those dedicated to cartoons.

Here are the main ones:

- aljazeerah.info, an Arab-American site that has included a section on 'Arab cartoons' since April 2002;
- arabcartoon.net (http://www.arabcartoon.net), a new site that proposes a lot of cartoonists;
- iviews.com, an American site 'devoted to Muslim causes' that publishes the cartoons of Khalil Bendib (see also www.bendib.com);
- Palestine media watch (www.pmwatch.org), a site that gives access to Palestinian cartoonist sites;
- Arabia.com (www.arabia.com/cartoonopia/english), a Jordanian site that used to edit and archive drawings by some twelve cartoonists in the Arab region: the Palestinian Imad Hajjaj (*Al Rai*, Jordan), the Lebanese Stravro Jabra (*Daily Star*), the Lebanese Mahmoud Kahil (*Asharq Al-Awsat*, *Arab News*, *Al-Majalla Arab news*, Saudi Arabia), the Palestinian Abu Arafeh (*Al Quds*), the Palestinian woman cartoonist, Omayya Joha (*Al Quds*), the Indonesian Steff, two Palestinians Ba'ha Bukhari (formerly at *Al Duds*, East Jerusalem, now at *Al-Ayyam* in Ramallah) and Nasser Al-Ja'afari (Palestine), Abdel Azis Sadeq in Qatar, Rabee in Saudi, the Jordanian, Majed Rasmy, the Egyptian Bahgori.

- A number of them have their own sites, such as Ba'ha (www. Bah-cartoon.net/indexl), Imad Hajjaj (www.baladna.com), Abu Arafeh (www.abuarafeh.com) as well as Omayya Joha (www.omayya.com); dozens of Palestinian sites, such as Intifada.com, or the official press site of the Palestinian Authority, where cartoons by Zaid are posted (www.ipc.gov.ps);
- Islam Belgique (www.islambelgique.com/caricature.cfm), a site that shows film cartoons taken from the aljzeera.com site (www.aljazeera.net/Cartoons);
- Certain 'anti-globalisation' sites such as Indymedia.com, where cartoons by the Brazilian Latuff are posted;
- *Al Ahram Weekly Online* runs cartoons by the Egyptian, Gomaa Farahat, who also works for the satirical weekly Rose al Youssef;
- Middle East Media Research Institute (MEMRI), as well as *Palestinian Media Watch* or *Intelligence and Terrorism Information Center* are also very interesting sites.

In many cases it has unfortunately been impossible to establish the date of a cartoon.

We have also consulted the bulletins on Arab cartoons issued periodically by the *Anti-Defamation League* and finally, for the period prior to 1998, the work of Arie Stav, *Peace: The Arabian Caricature. A Study of Anti-Semitic Imagery* (Jerusalem and New York: Gefen Publishing House, 1999).

First, we should like to thank our friend Dr Simon Cohen for his kindness in urging us to translate our book and to our English Publishers Frank and Stewart Cass. We should like to offer our thanks once again to Emmanuelle Kotek and Pascale Gruber who agreed to read through the manuscript; to Jérome Aubignat, archivist at the Centre de

Documentation Juive Contemporaine de Paris, Corinne Guichart & Alain Steinberg our wonderful graphists, Esther Webman at the Stephen Roth Institute for the Study of Antisemitism and Racism at the University of Tel Aviv, Simi Epstein of the Vidal Sassoon Centre at the Hebrew University of Jerusalem, as well as Elie Kasparian for his translation work, Vincent Decaestecker, Yves Frey and Myriam Glikerman. This study would not have been possible without the financial support of the Evens Foundation (many thanks to Dr. Jacques Ehelberg & Jan Morrens), Richard Laub, president of the Hermansohn Foundation and Danièle and Michel Wajs. Finally we want to thank Didier Pasamonix, specialist in Jewish strip cartoons, Julian Voloj Dessauer former president of EUJS, who gave us all the material distributed during the 'anti-racist' conference in Durban (WCAR), *Cousin* Leon Saltiel for the surprising Greek caricatures and of course my brother Daniel. Last but not least, this book would not have been possible without the friendly collaboration of our cartoonists, who with very few exceptions permitted us to reproduce their work, or without Alisa Jaffa, our talented translator.

One of the primary forms of antisemitism is that of demonological anti-Judaism, that maintains Judaism is a conspiratorial organisation in the service of evil, relentlessly plotting the ruin of the human race. Since the Middle Ages the Talmud has been perceived as the ultimate work of evil. In fact all it consists of is commentaries. The Pope in *Al-Hayat al-Jadida*, 22 March 2000
The Pope: *'Peace on Earth!'*
Satanic Jew: *'Colonies on Earth!'* He has written on him: *'Israeli colonialism'*

*'The book of Judah. It was the Devil himself that wrote the Talmud with the blood
and the tears of non-Jews', Der Stürmer, Nuremberg, August 1936*

Two old and still vivid 'antisemyths': crucifixion and infanticide

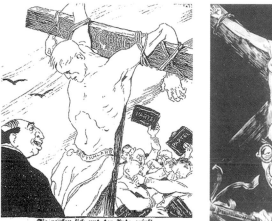

One of the paintings that depict the so-called murder of a Christian child by Jews in Sandomierz (Poland)

There were no limits to the subjects exploited by Nazi propaganda – even the Crucifixion. The first drawing refers to the Young Plan (August 1930); the second to the frenzied antisemitic erotic phantasies of Dr Kurt Plischke (1930)

The Jews refuse to hand over the thirty pieces of silver to the Arab leaders that were the ones to betray Palestine/Christ.
Al-Istiqlal (Palestine), 1 June 2001

Sharon Crucifying Peace
Nagi, *Al Ahram* (Egypt), 27 October 2004

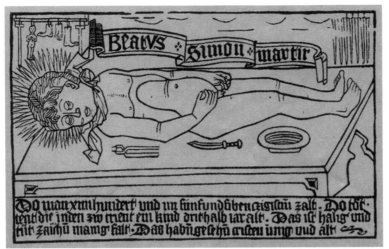

The case of little Simon, the infant believed to have been murdered by the Jews of Trent (Italy) in 1475, stands out as a classic example of what was believed to be a ritual murder. Shortly before Simon went missing, Bernardo da Feltre, an itinerant Franciscan preacher, had delivered a series of sermons in Trent in which he vilified the local Jewish community. When Simon went missing around Easter, 1475, his father thought that he must have been kidnapped and murdered by Jews. The leaders of the Jewish community were arrested, and seventeen of them confessed under torture. Toward the end of June, eight of the wealthiest Jews, after receiving baptism, were put to death, some being burned at the stake and the rest beheaded. Meanwhile Simon became a focus of veneration for the local Catholic Church. Over one hundred miracles were directly attributed to 'Little Saint Simon' within a year of his disappearance, and his cult spread across Italy, Austria and Germany. His veneration was confirmed (equivalent to beatification) in 1588 by Pope Sixtus V and he was considered a martyr and a patron of kidnap and torture victims.

Picture taken from Susana Buttaroni and Stanislaw Musial (ed), *Ritual Murder: Legend in European History* (Krakow and Nuremberg-Frankfurt: Association for Cultural Initiatives, 2003)

The last trial against ritual murder was held in Russia in 1911. This event inspired Bernard Malamud who described it in his novel The Fixer, (New York, 1966). In Kiev, Mendel Meilis, a young factory director is arrested for a ritual crime. This is one of the handbills distributed during the trial featuring 'the little martyr' Andrei Touchinsky. Its aim was to urge parents to take special care of their children during the Jewish Easter.

Al Jafari, *Arabia.com* (Jordan), 22 May 2001

Chapter 1

The prevailing myth in the Christian West from 1144 to 1946: The vampire, cannibal and child-slaughtering Jew

By way of introduction: three 'antisemyths'

In Western Europe from the twelfth century onwards a policy took hold of systematically outlawing the Jews from society, as myths were spread concerning their satanic nature.[8] They were commonly portrayed displaying the attributes of the Devil – a tail, horns and cloven hooves.[9] In particular the Jews indulged in the practice of slaughtering Christian children as part of skilfully programmed[10] rituals, sometimes to replay the crucifixion of Jesus (ritual murder), sometimes to drink their blood or steal their organs (blood libel).[11] The accusation levelled at them was that the Jews would kill Christian children in order to obtain the 'Christian blood' allegedly required for the baking of the unleavened bread eaten at Passover, or for other religious rites. Even when the higher ranks of the clergy often expressed their opposition to such rumours, they nevertheless persisted in popular belief, supported and encouraged by local clergy, who turned the location of the alleged murders into places of pilgrimage.

The French historian, Jean Delumeau,[12] considers the myth of the Jew as cannibal one of the great 'fears' of the Christian West during the Middle Ages and the Renaissance, along with witches, the Devil or the plague. The origin of this fantasy can be traced back to the activity allotted early on to the Jews by the princes and the church – dealing in money. From money raking to bloodsucking is a short step. Hence the rumour that the Jews not only sucked the economic blood of the Christians through usury but they also fed on the blood of the Christian children they murdered. This explains how from this point on the image of the Jew will come to be inextricably associated with gold and with blood, and deicide will be considered on a par with usury. This image blends very conveniently into the symbolic figure of Judas – the Jew who took thirty pieces of silver as reward for treason. The famous nineteenth-century French historian, Jules Michelet, provides evidence of this in a passage not without antisemitic prejudice:

> In the Middle Ages the person who knows where to find gold, the true alchemist, and real sorcerer, is the Jew or the half-Jew, the Lombard. A prolific nation, that above all others, had the strength to grow in number, to breed, thereby increasing Jacob's flocks and Shylock's golden ducats. Persecuted, hunted and re-drafted throughout the whole of the Middle Ages, they performed the indispensable role of intermediary between tax collectors and their victims, pumping money out from below to render to the king on high, who received it with an ungracious grimace. Yet they they always had something left over for themselves… Patient, indestructible, they triumphed through

persistence. They solved the problem of making money disappear; enfranchised by bills of exchange, they were now free, they were now the masters; from repeated beatings and humiliation, they were now enthroned over the world. For the poor man to speak to the Jew, for him to approach his dark little house with its infamous reputation, to speak to this man, who, they say, crucifies little children, meant he had to be under extreme financial duress. Given the choice between financial duress that demanded the very core of his being and his blood, and the Devil that wanted his soul, he chose the Jew as the lesser of two evils. So that by the time he had exhausted his very last means of support, with his bed sold, his wife and children sleeping on the floor, shaking with fever or crying for bread, at that point, his head down and his body bent lower than if he had been carrying a load of timber, then he would slowly make for the accursed house, and stand at length in front of it, before

knocking. The Jew having cautiously opened the small grille, a strange and difficult dialogue would ensue. What did the Christian have to say? 'In the name of God'. 'The Jew killed your God!' 'For pity's sake.' 'When did a Christian ever take pity on a Jew? Those aren't the words I want. What I want is a pledge.' 'What pledge can a man give who has nothing?' To which the Jew would softly reply:

My friend, in accordance with the edict of the king, our sire, I do not lend either against a bloodstained cloak nor against an iron plough... no, there has to be a pledge, and it has to be yourself. I am not one of you, my law is not the Christian law. It is far more ancient (*in partes secanto*). Your flesh will serve. Blood for gold, a life for a life. A pound of your flesh that I will nourish with my gold, just one pound of your fine flesh. The gold lent by the murderer of the Son of God can be nothing but mur-

In 1965, in the wake of the Second Vatican Council, the Catholic Church began to reinvestigate the story of Saint Simon and opened the trial records anew. Finally declaring the episode a fraud, the cult of Saint Simon was supressed by Pope Paul VI and the shrine erected to him was dismantled. He was removed from the calendar, and his future veneration was forbidden, but some ultra-Catholics have ignored this suppression and continue to venerate the holy little boy of Trent.

Little Simon was finally withdrawn from the calendar (of saints) in 1966. Engraving, Illustration in Hartmann Schedel's *Weltchronik*, Germany, 1493.

derous gold, anti-divine, or as was said back in those days, Anti-Christ. So here is the gold of the Anti-Christ.

This Anti-Christ, this anti-god, must bring down God, that is to say, the Church: the traditional church, the priests, the pope; the regular church, the monks, the Templars.[13]

1144: Ritual murder

The accusation of ritual murder is recorded for the first time in 1144 in Norwich,[14] a town at the time home to one of the largest and most prosperous Jewish communities in England. The accusation was the product of the imagination of Thomas de Monmouth, and was supposed to provide a 'rational' explanation for the mysterious death of a young apprentice found in a wood the day before Good Friday.[15] The rumour that the boy had been murdered by the Jews spread like wildfire – the nearness of the Christian Easter aroused the latter to a frenzy of resentment and desire for revenge. Both the precise accusation as well as the crime had long been planned; a rabbinical conference that met in Narbonne, is said to have identified Norwich as a sacrificial site. So that from the twelfth century onwards, alongside the accusation of ritual murder, the myth emerged and became solidly entrenched of a secret society headed by a learned assembly of masked, conspiratorial rabbis, prefiguring the alleged 'Elders of Zion'[16] from the *Protocols* of the same name. Ritual murder and deicide are very distinctly linked.[17] If one were to believe the mother of the murdered boy and a priest, the young victim was taken by force to the synagogue in Norwich for a rehearsal of the Passion of Jesus. A very precise description states that the Jews placed a crown of thorns on the boy's head and then tied him to a tree. A judge was chosen to play the role of Pontius Pilate. Sentence was pronounced and the child was scourged until he loses consciousness. Covered with spittle, he was made to drink gall to cries of 'Christ – false prophet'. After which

he was crucified and his heart pierced with a lance. Even though the legal authorities hardly gave credence to these allegations – the local sheriff endeavoured to protect the threatened Jews from being lynched – the outcome was as might be expected. A distinguished Jew in the town was killed. He collapsed under the blows of a penniless petty nobleman, who just happened to be in debt to him.

The incident that left its mark on the popular imagination, led to the cult of St William; the relics of the apprentice became the focus of lasting pilgrimage. In fact, the motive of the clergy, in particular William de Turbeville, Bishop of Norwich (1146–74), to establish a *cultus* was probably pecuniary. Before any attempt at an autopsy as to how the boy met his death, the Prior tried to get the body for Lewes Priory, for he realised that it might become an object 'of conspicuous veneration and worship.' Thus attracting the valuable pilgrim trade by putting a martyr on display in his church.

The accusation of ritual murder soon spread through the whole of Europe like a powder trail – to Würzburg in 1147, to Blois in 1171 (where the entire Jewish community was burned alive), to Lincoln in 1255. There once again the murder was depicted as a re-enactment of the death of Christ on the Cross. It was related that '*the child had been fed in preparation for ten days beforehand and all the Jews of England were invited to his crucifixion.*' A century and a half later, by which time the last Jew had been expelled from the kingdom, the little martyr of Lincoln was to inspire Geoffrey Chaucer to end one of his *Canterbury Tales* (c.1390) with a prayer in memory of the child.

So, as I've said, as in and out the Jewry went
This little boy, he would sing out a song
And joyfully the notes rang out as
O Alma redemptoris he loudly sang.
Bringing Christ's dear Mother straight into his heart
And to her did he pray
Singing all the while as he went on his way.

Crucifixion of William of Norwich. Immediately after his death he was popularly venerated as a martyr and was soon regarded as a local saint in Norwich after miracles were attributed to him. The motive of the clergy, in particular William de Turbeville, Bishop of Norwich (1146–74), to establish a cultus was probably pecuniary. De Turbeville encouraged Thomas of Monmouth, a Benedictine monk who lived in Norwich to write *The Life and Miracles of St William of Norwich*. Monmouth was contemporary to the events he describes. His Latin work written about 1173 is the source of all subsequent folklore and myth upon William of Norwich.

Who lurking hidden in an alleyway
As the child went by at an even pace.
This cursed Jew seized the child and held him fast
Having cut his throat he cast him in a pit.

I say that in a wardrobe they threw him
And into it the Jews relieved their entrails.
O cursed folk of Herod, reborn
What do you think your evil intent avails?
Murder will out, certain it is, and never fails,
Especially when God's honour needs to be avenged.
Blood cries out on your accursed deeds. [...]

With no time lost the provost served all the Jews
With torture and shameful death
Who knew about the murder and that anon;
He would not swerve from justice to the villains.
'Evil shall be given to him that evil does deserve.'

Norwich Cathedral. Illustration taken from Buttaroni and Musial (eds), op. cit.

Our greatest foe, the serpent Satan
With his hornets nest in the heart of the Jew
Puffed up with rage saying:
'Oh Hebrew people, alas!
Do you find it right and good
That such a lad walks here singing out
The contrary to the teachings you revere?'
From that time on the Jews conspired
To chase from this world the innocent child;
An assassin they found and hired,

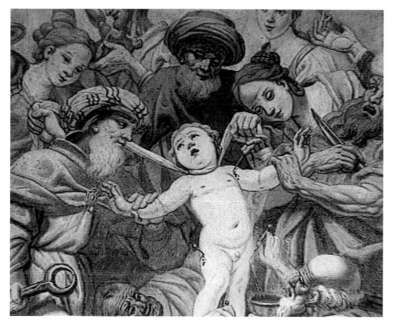

Wall painting in the former Church of Simon

So he had them dragged by wild horses
And then hung as the law requires. [...]

Oh you young Hugh of Lincoln, also slain by cursed Jews,
As all know well since it was not long ago,
Do you pray for us, sinful and weak, who ask,
That, of his mercy God will still let fall
Something of grace, and mercy multiply
For the dignity of his dear mother on high. Amen.[18]

The case of little Simon, the infant believed to have been murdered by the Jews of Trent in 1475, stands out as a classic example of what was believed to be a ritual murder. On Holy Thursday of the year 1475, the little child, then about 20 months old, son of a gardener, was missed by its parents. On the evening of Easter Sunday the body was found in a ditch. The leaders of the Jewish community were arrested, and seven-

teen of them confessed under torture. Fifteen of them, including Samuel, the head of the community, were sentenced to death and burned at the stake. Meanwhile Simon became the focus of veneration for the local Catholic Church. Over one hundred miracles were directly attributed to 'Little Saint Simon' within a year of his disappearance, and his cult spread across Italy and Germany. His *cultus* was confirmed (equivalent to beatification) in 1588 by Pope Sixtus V and he was considered a martyr and a patron of kidnap and torture victims. The trials against the Jews in Trent (1475) represent a turning-point in the relationship between Judaism and Christianity at the end of the Medieval era. The trials originated in a period of violent anti-Judaic polemics and broke with a longstanding indulgent attitude, particularly represented by the juridical literature of the Roman culture. The criminal proceedings undertaken against the Jews for murder due to contempt of the Christian faith formed a stereotype and was perpetuated in new forms, attitudes and tendencies which would worsen the juridical and social conditions of the Jewish people in the fifteenth century.

Simon of Trent (wooden sculpture),
in Buttaroni and Musial (eds), op. cit.

The stereotype of Jews committing ritual murder, acting out of their supposed 'hate for the Christian faith' was a belief particularly widespread in regions north of the Alps and within the German community in Trent. Here, the horrible accusations found general credence, without encountering any particular resistance, even among the highest political and ecclesiastical authorities. The main promoters of Simon's

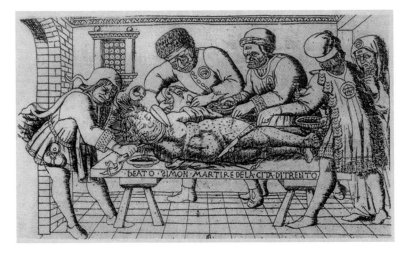

The ritual murder of Simon of Trent. Engraving, in Buttaroni and Musial (eds), op. cit.

cult were above all the bishop-prince of Trent, Giovanni Hinderbach, as well as those Franciscan preachers most fervid in their antisemitic campaign, such as Bernardino da Feltre and Michele Carcano. Simon's story was diffused along several channels: the Franciscan preaching, a vast number of treatises and tracts by jurists and humanists, as well as through woodcuts depicting the atrocity in graphic detail (it is worth noting that the art of printing at Trent began with the recounting of the martyrdom of little Simon in the German language illustrated with some of these images).[19] The diffusion of propaganda reached areas very distant from Trent and made a powerful impact on 'public opinion'. In 1912 a Catholic scholar, Abbé Elphège Vacandard, concluded that *'not a single case [of ritual murder] has ever been historically established'*, but it was only in 1965, in the wake of the Second Vatican Council, that the Church began to reinvestigate the story of Saint Simon and opened the trial records anew. Finally declaring the episode a fraud, the cult of Saint Simon was disbanded by Pope Paul VI and the shrine erected to him was dismantled. He was removed from the calendar, and his future veneration was forbidden.[20]

1150: Desecration of the Hosts

From the twelfth century onwards rumours began to circulate asserting that the Jews steal, deform or burn the Host in order to kill Jesus over again. This gave rise to a sinister legend that was to grow after the Lateran Council of 1215 consecrating the Eucharist.

In one of the first versions of this myth, the work of one Jean d'Outremeuse,[21] a chronicler from Liège, the story takes place in Cologne in 1150. Having been desecrated and buried by the Jews, the Host gave birth to a child; a priest disinterred it, whereupon it flew up to the skies bathed in a flood of ineffable light… The miracle constitutes an integral part of the Myth: the defaced Host bleeds, thereby proving the validity of the doctrine and the truth of the Christian faith.

Here and there throughout Europe consecrated Hosts were recovered stained with 'blood'.[22] On every occasion the Jews were accused of having pierced them with nails, which miraculously made them bleed. The desecration of the Host, which the Christians identify with Christ himself, amounted to a repetition of the crime that took place on Calvary. In 1370 some twenty Jews were burned alive in Brussels. In his *History of the Jews of Belgium*, Salomon Ullman relates the martyrdom of the Jews of Brussels:

A certain Jonathan from the Jewish community of Enghien used money to win over a Jew baptised in Louvain but living in Brussels and get him to agree to steal some Hosts from the church of Saint Catherine and bring them to Enghien. From

Le jour du Vendredi Saint l'an 1370 les chefs de la synagogue percèrent avec des poignards les Saintes Hosties volées dans une église et qu'ils avaient reçues de la veuve Jonathas. Le sang en jaillit et les juifs épouvantés tombèrent à la renverse, les habits teints du Sang miraculeux.

Depuis les miracles du T. S. Sacrement, la dévotion et l'amour des Bruxellois pour Lui ne se sont jamais ralentis pendant plusieurs siècles. Les grandes processions organisées aux anniversaires solennels attirèrent à Bruxelles beaucoup de monde; on construisit une quinzaine d'arcs de triomphe. Le défilé se prolongeait pendant six heures et quelquefois même on était obligé d'en remettre une partie au lendemain, et les fêtes se continuaient pendant 8 jours.

Bruxelles a mis au service du S. Sacrement de miracle le beau temple de Ste Gudule, on a consacré à sa gloire tout ce que l'art, la science et l'amour ont de plus beau pour dire aux siècles futurs sa foi et sa dévotion au T. S. Sacrement.

Blood, as ever!

The Cathedral of Saints Michel-and-Gudule: a monument used to exploit a judeophobic legend

Three images from the 'strip cartoon' inspired by the images of Epinal, recounting 'The Miracle of the hosts of Brussels' and marked *Propagande salésienne – oeuvre de Saint-Jean Bosco, 5 rue des Wallons à Liège (published by Gordinne, Liège, c. 1900, Didier Pasamonik collection)*

Enghien they were to be brought back to Brussels. After allegedly desecrating the Hosts, and fearing divine retribution, the Jews arranged to meet on 12 April 1370 in their synagogue in order to have the bleeding Hosts taken to Cologne by a woman; but she alerted the authorities to the Jews' intentions. The news of the alleged theft from the church set the entire population into a fury; they rose up, with the clergy at their head and set upon exterminating the Jews. Many of them succeeded in fleeing to avoid a wretched death; those who remained were thrown into prison or subjected to torture. After the prisoners had 'confessed' to taking part in the crime they were led in front of the church, where the theft of the Hosts had taken place, and there they were burned alive on 20 May 1370.[23]

The main stained-glass window in Brussels Cathedral

Il croyait ainsi s'en défaire et calmer sa femme épouvantée. Mais quelle ne fut pas sa terreur quand l'Hostie miraculeuse s'éleva intacte du milieu des flammes et voltigea çà et là par la chambre.

De plus en plus furieux, il l'attache à un poteau, la frappe de verges, veut la couper en morceaux. Vains efforts, elle demeure entière. Digne fils de ses pères, ne voulant lui épargner aucun outrage, le Juif la porte dans un lieu infect et la perce d'un coup de lance.

Poussé par une fureur satanique, le scélérat reprend la blanche Hostie et la jette dans une chaudière d'eau bouillante. O prodige! cette eau devient du sang, et la figure du Sauveur crucifié apparaît au Juif, à sa femme, à ses enfants. L'Hostie était donc vraiment Dieu. Le misérable allait être châtié.

A cette nouvelle, le peuple envahit la maison du Juif. Conduit prisonnier avec sa famille, Jonathas avoua toutes les circonstances du crime. Il fut condamné par le roi à être brûlé vif. Le malheureux n'eut pas un mot de repentir; mais sa femme et ses enfants, s'étant convertis, reçurent le baptême.

Miracle of Billettes in Paris (1290)

Four extracts from the 'strip cartoon' inspired by the images of Epinal, recounting 'The Miracle of Billettes in Paris, the Host crucified by a Jew' 9 no.725) and marked 'approved by the church'. These images of Epinal record a chronicle of Saint-Denis, which was the origin of the foundation of the church and the cloister of Billettes in Paris in 1427, the site of which is in the rue des Archives today in the fourth arrondissement in Paris (Liège, published by Gordinne, c. 1900. Didier Pasamonik collection).

E. C. Propagande Salésienne - Œuvre de St Jean Bosco - 59, Rue des Wallons, Liége.

Avec l'approbation ecclésiastique.

One can read that *This strip is 'published with church approval'.*

The Jews were banished from the Duchy of Brabant. As for the 'miracle' of the Hosts, it was subsequently represented on ten of the fifteen stained-glass windows of the Cathedral of Saints Michael-and-Gudule. 'It is distressing to think,' reflects Didier Pasamonik, 'that no Belgian king, and not a single princely marriage were consecrated, without just by raising their heads, seeing these dreadful images of hateful Jews stabbing the bleeding Hosts.'[24]

1235 Blood libel

If at the time when the first accusations of infanticide were made, circumcision or crucifixion were mentioned, the intent to dehumanise the enemy soon acquired the ultimate horror of cannibalism, that is to say the most inhuman of the three 'fundamental crimes' listed by René Girard in his work, *Le bouc émissaire* (*The Scapegoat*), after 'crimes of violence', such as parricide or infanticide, and 'sexual crimes', such as incest, rape or bestiality.[25] The accusation of cannibalism appears for

Alleged ritual murder of Rinn. This fresco that remained until 1994 on the vault of the St Andrew the Apostle church in Judenstein, near Rinn. Picture taken from Buttaroni and Musial (eds), op. cit.

Some years before the alleged ritual murder of the 'Blessed Simonino' in Trent, a similar allegation which cannot be historically proven led, however, to similar accusations against Jews. About 1620, Hyppolitus Guarinonius, an overzealous monastery doctor in Hall, started to create a whole biography around the nameless and faceless 'child of Rinn'. When his zealous efforts to collect all the necessary information from the region adjacent to Rinn finally failed, he constructed a purely hypothetical destiny: the family names of the parents of the child of Rinn's, his own name (Andreas), the year, month and day of his birth and his death as well as the circumstances and 'peculiarities' of his 'martyrdom' were all pure fiction.

the first time in Germany, in Fulda in 1235. When the five children of a Christian miller were found dead, the rumour quickly spread that two Jews had killed them; a frenzied crowd, brandishing a crucifix, attacked the town and slit the throats of thirty Jewish families. The affair caused such an uproar that the Emperor Frederick II, the great opponent of Pope Innocent IV (1243–54), called a commission of Jews who had converted to Christianity: they excluded the possibility of such a crime (1236). Nevertheless the accusations by no means ceased – almost every year, with the approach of Easter, a mysterious murder would come to light in some place or other, and instantly suspicion would fall on the Jews. Pope

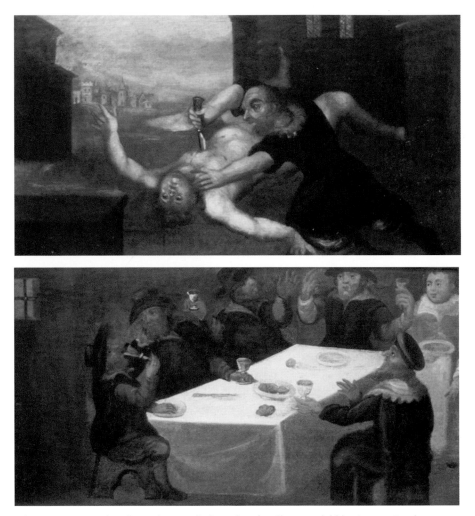

The two paintings that depict the so-called murder of a Christian child by Jews in Sandomierz, a small town in southeastern Poland, can be still seen in the St Paul's Church presbytery. They belong to the Charles Gabriel de Prévot cycle (1710). These tales were popularised in two notorious books published contemporaneously by the local priest, Stefan Zuchowski, instigator of one of the trials of Jews for such alleged crimes and commissioner of the paintings.

Innocent IV reacted too against the case of a girl murdered in Valreas and the upheaval that followed (1247). In two bulls, he pointed out the cruelty of the legal procedures which had followed the murder. In one of the bulls, he wrote:

We have heard the bitter complaints of the Jews, who are smeared with abject calumnies to provide a pretext to attack them and pillage their belongings. When the corpse of a murdered man is found, they are held responsible. Without

Ritual murder. Painting in Sandomierz Cathedral

The Sandomierz Cathedral

This painting in the cathedral church in Sandomierz, formerly known as *Infanticidia* or 'Ritual Murder by Jews', is said to commemorate a ritual murder perpetrated by Jews in 1710. Stefan Zuchowski financed this painting by French painter Charles Gabriel de Prévot. It portrays the episode as Zuchowski imagined it. The scene corresponds to the sequence related in his book *Process kryminalny [A Criminal Trial]*: a Christian woman's offering of the child to the Jews; torture of the child in a barrel lined with protruding nails; extraction of the child's blood; and the culminating scene of the child's body devoured and then vomited out by a dog. This image is a vivid instance both of the Catholic perception of Jewish hostility toward Christians and also of Catholic anti-Jewish sentiments in the pre-modern period. Following the restoration of diplomatic relations between Poland and Israel in the 1990s and the appointment of a Jewish–Catholic committee on reconciliation, a demand arose that this painting be removed from the church, as other paintings of this sort had been in Poland, as in Kalwaria Zebrzydowska, near Pope John Paul's hometown of Wadowice. The painting was kept in place but a new description was added, reading 'The alleged ritual murder by Jews'.

any recourse to law, innocent people are thrown into prison, are tortured and condemned to a shameful death. Thus the Jews are made to suffer at the hands of present-day lords and monarchs even more than their ancestors suffered in Egypt under the Pharaohs. Forbidding the persecution of the Jews, whose return [to the Christian faith] merciful God awaits, we command you to treat them benevolently. Should the Jews again be illegally oppressed by the church, the nobility or officialdom, you must not tolerate this.

Innocent IV ruled that the imprisoned Jews should be released and those who had suffered damages should be compensated; from now on all should be given the right to live unharmed. He also provided the motives for his reaction: first of all, Jews could convert to Christianity. Moreover, the Lord wanted them to survive because they were the first witnesses to his passion and resurrection and they remain 'tribute-payers to Christianity' – by keeping the biblical books they contribute to the preservation of the origins of Christianity and point towards Christianity with their behaviour. To the traditional *Sicut Judaeis* bull of former Popes, Innocent added a clause against all accusations of the use of blood for ritual purposes. The case of Fulda was mentioned, and both there and in a fourth text written for the bishops of Germany and France, clear prescriptions from the Old Testament Law were quoted as proof that Jews could not commit such crimes.

To no effect, it has to be said.[26]

As Leon Poliakov has pointed out, it is in this definitive version that the myth of ritual murder emerges as the keystone of anti-Jewish thought.[27] Initially it relates to a Christian rite – the Passion – and not to the Jewish Passover – where stolen blood (or even organs such as the heart or the liver) is used

Infanticide again, depicted here as a Jewish ritual. Eighteenth-century French engraving after a German work showing the ritual murder of six Christian children in Regensburg in 1476.

for magical purposes during a secret ceremony enacting the killing of Christ (in the flesh or by use of an effigy).

With the blood libel, the symbolic elements are immutably put into place that will constitute the 'dramatisation' of all cases of this kind over the centuries – repetition of crimes (Easter time), their practical function (baking of unleavened bread), with its specific ritual and programme. Further, there is the fact that among the relevant witnesses figuring in these stories, there is nearly always a renegade, recently baptised Jew. The monk Theobald of Cambridge, a baptised Jew, is the one to endorse the first case. Taking advantage of his Jewish origins, he is the one to provide most of the details relating to the crime and its manner of execution – details that will recur unflaggingly over the course of time. The purpose of the crime is to procure Christian blood to be mixed in with the batter used to prepare unleavened bread. The young victim is bled white. If there is more blood than required for the unleavened Passover bread, the excess is stored in vessels. The dried blood is later distributed and sold to Jewish communities who store it and rehydrate it before use.[28]

It is worth noting the absurdity and paradox of this accusation, as in the words of Daniel Tollet[29] it overlooks the Biblical prohibition on touching blood: *And whatsoever man there be of the House of Israel, or of the strangers that sojourn among them, that eateth any manner of blood, I will set my face against that soul that eateth blood, and will cut him off from among his people.*[30]

Furthermore not only does Judaism condemn murder, but since the destruction of the Temple in 70 CE animal sacrifice has also been prohibited.[31] All to no avail. On the contrary, as observed by the historian, Pierre Chaunu:

Engraved wood, Poland, c.1900
A new twist on the old accusation: the Jews suck blood directly
from their young victim, making them real vampires

The fact that the accusation in whatever instance is totally implausible without any attempt at proof does nothing to diminish its effectiveness – quite the contrary. The strength of the Judaeophobic argument stems from the very fact that the Jewish religious ethic has an absolute horror of blood in general, and even more so of the blood of small children, so that Adonay, the Eternal accuses the pagan gods and those that they tempt to perform this abomination ... the accusation is the more effective by accusing the victim of indulging in a crime that the Jews claim to abominate and that in fact they abominate above all others.[32]

The myth of the Jew as a child-murderer spread all over Europe, from Germany to Spain, from France to Flanders, from Switzerland to Poland,[33] right up to the middle of the twentieth century, as we shall see, with the pogrom of Kielce in Poland in 1946. Along with Jews settling in the Middle Ages in Poland, came stories of alleged ritual murders committed by them in the countries of Western Europe. Already during the reign of Kazimierz the Great, Jonas Mordachai, grandfather of the well-known Esterka, the King's lover, had been accused of a ritual murder in Opoczno. The first legal proceeding of ritual murder within the lands of the Republic of Poland occurred however in Rawa (Mazowiecka province) in 1547, and the last in Olkusz in 1787. According to Jacek Wijaczka, there were a

total of 100 accusations and legal trials for ritual murder within the lands of the Republic of Poland.[34]

Desecration of the Host, ritual murder and blood libels were to become the leitmotif of charges against the Jews, perpetuating the idea of the evil and inhumane nature of the Jews and inciting the Christian populations to take revenge for their alleged crimes. Immediately a Christian child disappears, immediately a body is found in a wood or in a river, the rabble accuses the Jews. Sometimes they accuse them of having crucified a Christian child, sometimes of having bled him or extracted his entrails for the production of the special bread consumed during the Jewish Passover (unleavened bread or matzos). The two charges were very often combined. In 1294 all the Jews of the city of Berne were expelled following the disappearance of a young boy. Two and a half centuries later a fountain was erected on the Place de la Grenette and named *Kinderfresserbrunnen* (Child-eater's fountain). It portrays an ogre wearing a pointed yellow hat (sumptuary laws of dress restrictions were imposed on the Jews in the Middle Ages),

Polish antisemitic postcard (1899) regarding the Hilsner affair. The image appears on an American Nazi website (*screwdriver.net*) emphasising the importance of human sacrifice in the Jewish tradition.

13

Dreyfus and Hilsner: two victims of modern antisemitism,[36]
Zola and Masaryk: two champions of judicial truth.

pushing some children seized by him into a sack, and displaying sadistic pleasure as he consumes one of his little victims. To this very day the fountain is regularly repainted and restored.

Between 1867 and 1914 there were no less than twelve trials for ritual murder in the German-speaking countries alone. The most renowned by far was that of Leopold Hilsner, a young Jew from Czechoslovakia, then part of the Austro-Hungarian empire.

Hilsner's troubles began on Easter Saturday, 1 April 1899 in a forest in the neighbourhood of the village of Polna in the Bohemian highlands. The body of a 19-year old seamstress, Anezka Hruzova was found here, after she had been missing since 29 March. To some of the villagers the deep gash in the victim's throat suggested the method of slaughtering cattle employed by Jewish butchers. Hilsner was charged with the crime.

His trial began in a climate of collective antisemitic hysteria that has gone down in history as the 'hilsneriade'. Tomas Masaryk, later to become the first President of Czechoslovakia, saved the accused from the death sentence, but Hilsner remained condemned in perpetuity. Pardoned in 1918 by Charles I, the last Austro-Hungarian Emperor, he died ten years later in Vienna. Polna today is a sleepy little village. The tourist trail always leads to the site of the crime, where a wooden cross has recently been put up. It goes without saying that Hilsner was innocent – in 1968 Anezka's brother confessed on his deathbed that he had killed his sister in order to steal her money. A sad conclusion to one of the most

infamous miscarriages of justice of the twentieth century. The Hilsner affair earned Masaryk the hatred and distrust of many of his fellow citizens, with some of his own friends even turning against him. It affected Masaryk so deeply that he considered leaving the country, but fortunately his wife persuaded him not to. Masaryk confided in the writer Karel Capek that the 'hilsneriade' was *one of the most difficult issues of his life, but that it was not without its recompense because as a result the Jewish press supported him during the war*.

The last of the major ritual murder cases – the Beilis Affair – occurred further east, in the Russian Empire, in Kiev to be exact. Unlike Hilsner, the accused Mendel Beilis was acquitted after a two-year hearing and a campaign of international support.

Gold and Blood
At the centre of the antisemitic discourse

The first Catholic antisemitic newspaper appeared in France in 1882. Its founder was one Abbé Chabauty. Then in 1886 two novels with provocative titles were published: *The Countess Shylock* by G. d'Orget and *The Vampire Baron* by Guy de Charnacé. At the same time in Germany Canon Rohling published *Talmudjude (The Talmud Jew)*, a work centred on the age-old theme of ritual murder, which was to have widespread distri-

Birds of the Night by Bobb, in La Silhouette, 16 January 1898.
Reinach, defence counsel for Dreyfus, is drawn as a vampire
(enlarged detail)

The United States prevented by one of their own from intervening on behalf of the Cubans in revolt against the Spanish Crown, as Rothschild insists on repayment of his loan in the form of children's blood.

bution throughout Europe. Three separate editions translated into French appeared in the year 1899, one of which by Father Maximilien de Lamarque was published in Brussels.[36] The myth of the Jew as a drinker of blood, as stressed by Guy Jucquois and Pierre Sauvage, was to have a protracted life. Although no material evidence has ever been produced in corroboration, the major theological dictionaries and Catholic apologetics from the late nineteenth century and the first half of the twentieth century went to great lengths to scrutinise painstakingly the alleged proofs and to consider the 'milder' forms of ritual murder.[37] The subject of the money- and blood-sucking Jew features regularly in the cartoons of this period.

France is at the centre of this rumour. Sorlin's classic study of the antisemitism of the clergy and the Catholic believers in France at the end of the nineteenth century just makes one wonder. It shows the extent to which this belief is widely and consistently expressed in the publications of *La Bonne Presse*, and in particular in the daily *La Croix*:

'The publication of "scientific" works on the subject,' writes Sorlin, *'[reinforce the editors] in their sentiment; but above all the fact that the Church has "placed on its altars one of the victims of Jewish fanaticism" strikes them as the ultimate proof; the Church has spoken, no doubt remains [...] From 1875 to 1899 La Bonne Presse discovered some twenty Jewish crimes; it noted that most of the press never referred to them; a conspiracy of silence, supported by Jewish gold, enveloped these horrors; La Croix feels bound to insist and not ignore the slightest clue; the more the Jews counter with denial, the more the paper asserts its viewpoint.*[58] It is worth pointing out that in 1890 *La Croix*, the organ of the French Assumptionists, claims to be *'the most anti-Jewish paper in France'*. The Assumptionists are in no doubt whatsoever that the Jews are Devil worshippers and are always hatching conspiracies: *'the Jews form themselves into a secret society, governed by an occult leader, the Society of the Sons of the Widow. The Widow is Jerusalem deprived of her Temple [...] This society has as its aim the destruction of the kingdom of Jesus Christ.*[39]

The means of achieving this is money. The Jews control the banks. Gold is the source of their evil power. Consequently it is clear why the notion of ritual murder, and belief in a Jewish secret society that is both to order the crime

One of the first forms of antisemitism maintains that Judaism is a conspiratorial organisation in the service of evil (Germany, 1930). Cartoon published in Kurt Plischke's book, *The Jew, as a racial contaminant: a charge against the Jews and a warning to Germany's women and girls.* 2nd édition, Berlin: Schöneberg Verlag, Deutsche Kultur-Wacht.

Das größte Getreide-Wucherthier der Welt.

'The biggest usurer in the world'. The multiple faces of the all-powerful Jew, varying from vampire, to dragon, poisonous toadstool, or plague carrier. *Kikeriki*, Vienna, c.1910

1930

EL GOBIERNO
MUNDIAL INVISIBLE
o
EL PROGRAMA JUDIO
PARA SUBYUGAR AL
MUNDO

Spanish edition of *the Protocols*: 'The invisible Jewish world government or the Jewish programme for world domination', 1930

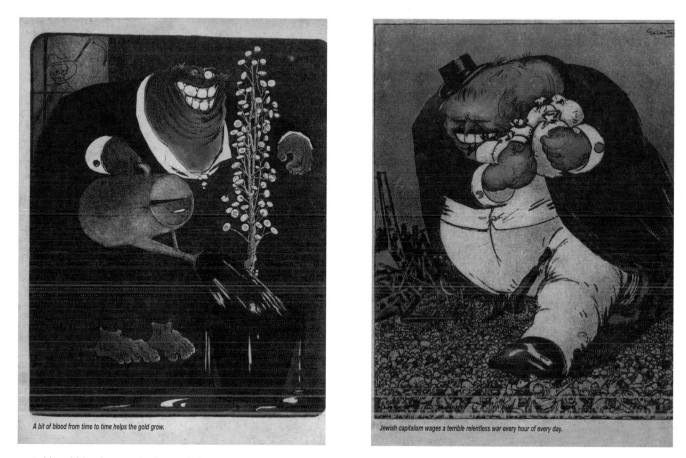

A bit of blood from time to time helps the gold grow.

Jewish capitalism wages a terrible relentless war every hour of every day.

Gold and blood are at the heart of classic antisemitic imagery going back to the Middle Ages. The Jew feeds on money as well as on the blood of Christians. Harking back to the myth of Jewish usury, the nineteenth century adds on the theme of the Jew as a warmonger. The Jew needs blood and war to make his gold yield profit. Shown here are two cartoons by the Italian Gabriele Galantara, in *L'Assiette au beurre* (Paris), special issue 'Vive l'Angleterre', 1907, no.324. Joël Kotek collection.

La Déchristianisation de la France

Antisemitic postcard from Brittany opposing the Jew-ridden French Republic. This is represented by a hideous-looking woman with a hooked nose, holding out a Star of David, while politicians are pushing to trample on the body of Christ in front of displeased Catholic Bretons. Modern republicanism is here portrayed as a Jewish invention: a Jewish vampire dominates a Jew-ridden France.

(Jewish) Bat, *Der Stürmer*, Germany

Affair, the book by John Grand-Carteret that appeared in 1898, half of which consisted of foreign cartoons, indicate the growing international awareness of cartoonists who must have known what was going on beyond their own frontiers. A year on from this publication, a similar anthology appeared in Berlin, consisting mainly of cartoons from central and eastern Europe. Given that antisemitic cartoons so readily crossed national borders, some of them outlasted the actual period of the affair to an astonishing extent.[41]

These myths were to spread throughout Europe right up to the middle of the twentieth century. Nazi propagandists and collaborators (cf. the French illustrated magazine, *Le Téméraire*) eager to supply additional evidence of the innate malevolence of the Jews, were naturally going to revive them.

The image of the Jew under the Nazis and collaborators

and to implement it, are inevitably going to be linked. A group of Jewish 'elders holding assemblies in some distant land will draw lots to appoint the location and the person to carry out the sacrifice.

The ultimate goal of the global Jewish conspiracy would be the establishment of the Kingdom of Israel, the global Jewish tyranny· '*Every human being is a potential victim of the Jews.*'[40]

From the nineteenth century to the mid-1930s the subject of Jewish gold inextricably linked with Christian blood was to hold sway from the United States to France by way of Austria. If antisemitism of the Nazi variety is the most virulent and consists of a level of violence and ignominy hitherto unequalled, we have to remember it was actually France with the Dreyfus Affair that unified the language and the codes of iconic antisemitism, employing massive dissemination of images to do so.

'*That was probably the moment,*' in the words of Marie-Anne Matard Bonucci, '*when certain antisemitic images that were destined to become universal, such as the Jew depicted as a spider in the middle of a web took permanent hold. The Dreyfus*

As Raul Hilberg has shown in his work on the destruction of the Jews of Europe,[41] for the Nazis it was Judaism in its entirety that dug its roots into criminality. The Jews constitute a pseudo-people bound by hereditary criminality. Presented in this way, their elimination becomes a necessity, useful for the evolution of humanity of the same order as capital punishment or preventive detention as a deterrent for other criminals. For thousands of years the Jews were capable of mass murder. By way of proof, Helmut Schramm, a Nazi 'researcher' assembled all the myths about ritual murders committed by the Jews in a 'scholarly' work, *Der jüdische Ritualmord: eine historische Untersuchung* (*Jewish Ritual Murder: a historical survey*). Himmler was so impressed by this that he immediately recommended it to Ernst Kaltenbrunner, his second-in-command in the SS. 'I have ordered multiple copies of this book,' he wrote. I shall distribute them among the Standartenführer (SS colonels). I am sending you several hundred copies to give to your Einsatzkommandos, and especially to those actively engaged in the Jewish question.'

'Kosher meat… pays well and costs little.' Cartoon by Ralph Soupault, one-time communist with a following of social antisemites. *Au Pilori*, no.112, 27 September 1940. The themes of blood and the Crucifixion were prominent in antisemitic propaganda in France too.

Georges Virebeau, *The Jews and their Crimes* (Paris: National Office of Propaganda, 1938), p.125.

Cover of an issue of *Defence of the Race* (1941), whose editor in chief, Giorgio Almirante, founded the neo-fascist Italian Social Movement (MSI).

'*Ritual Murder!*' Portrayal of the Jew as a child murderer and lover of blood is at the heart of Hitler's propaganda; here the Nazis attribute their own morbid drives to the Jews by the characteristic phenomenon of projection.

The Jewish plan to assassinate the non-Jews revealed!
Detail, *Der Stürmer*, May 1934

Ritual murder: the death of Gertrude Lenhoff, aged 10. *Der Stürmer*, undated.

The Jew yet again portrayed as a warmonger. The heading reads: *'Europe on the razor's edge'*, and the caption below: *'The Jews want war, people don't. The people bleed, the Jew is victorious.'* Der Stürmer, July 1934.

These are myths that kill! The work recommended by the head of the SS to Hitler's volunteer assassins consisted of a collection of stories about the murders the Jews were supposed to have inflicted on Christian children. As Hilberg points out, this is without doubt what attracted Himmler's interest in the work. He was to go so far as to order Kaltenbrummer to conduct research into 'the ritual murders in Romania, Hungary and Bulgaria. He suggested calling in the Security Police to search through tribunal records and British police registers for entries referring to children that had disappeared so that in our radio broadcasts to England we can state that a child has disappeared in village A or village B, and that this is without question a fresh case of Jewish ritual murder.'[42]

From Berlin to Pars, by way of Antwerp and Belgrade, the myth of the Jew in control, a drinker of blood was to be at the centre of the propaganda of hate.[43].

Graves of the last 42 European victims accused of ritual murder. The Kielce pogrom took place on 4 July 1946 when the townspeople accused a group of Holocaust survivors of hiding Christian children in the cellar of their building, dubbed 'the Kibbutz'. The fact that the building had no cellar did not prevent the police, assisted by the army from massacring the inhabitants of the building. The source of the tragedy was the running-away of a nine-year-old child, Henryk Blaszczyk, whose father forced him to transform his escapade into a kidnapping.

Chapter 2

The new Arab-Muslim Judeophobia

The myth of the Jew as a drinker of blood, central to Christendom until the collapse of Germany and even longer, as in Kielce in Poland in 1946, was largely unheard-of in Muslim lands. Regrettably it was to end up firmly entrenched in the those regions.

Since the establishment of the State of Israel, propagandists and cartoonists of the Arab-Muslim states have been drawing their inspiration from 'Christian' antisemitic and Nazi images. Sometimes they come up with original work of their own that goes much further.

Myths of Christian origin

The arguments dredged up from the classic armoury of Islamic anti-Judaism, such as 'perfidy' and 'treachery', the distrust associated with the *dhimmi* status, or 'protected'[44] of traditional Muslim society, have been progressively augmented by issues that might be considered as the prerogative of the Christian world. In this respect Bernard Lewis, the Islamic scholar, is the most outspoken: the persecutions in Islamic lands '*never took the form of Christian antisemitism: such as fear of a conspiracy of world Jewish domination, denunciation for associating with the Devil. The Jews were never accused either of poisoning the wells or spreading the plague, and even the charge of ritual murder was unknown until the new Greek subjects of the Ottoman Empire took them there in the fifteenth century.*'[45]

The accusation of deicide was likewise absent – from an Islamic viewpoint, this notion is altogether absurd, if not sacrilegious. Jesus was not God, but another of the Prophets.[46] For all that, could the Jews be content with their lot? Far from it.

If the Koran contains arguments justifying all kinds of attitudes towards the Jews, ranging from tolerance bordering on friendliness to the most pitiless hostility, its rejection of Judaism is nonetheless radical. Contrary to Christianity, Islam rejects the Torah, but nonetheless adapts the essence of its narrative for application to the new religion. Faced with the same problem of its origins as the early followers of Christ, and equally disappointed as the latter by the refusal of the Jews in Arab lands to accept him as the ultimate messenger predicted in the scriptures, Muhammad severs all links with Judaism. The extent of the break corresponds to his disappointment: the Jews – those at least that are not exterminated – are expelled from Medina and soon from the entire Arabian Peninsula. Instead of Jerusalem the Prophet selects Mecca as the orientation for prayer (*qibla*). This move prompts Muhammad to proclaim a theology of falsification by disclaiming the Jewishness of Abraham (allegedly already Muslim) and by presenting Ishmael, presumed to be the ancestor of the Arabs, as his true heir. The Jews and the Christians in turn are accused of nothing less than having falsified the word of God for their own interests. But while denying that Judaism and Christianity are in truth descended from Abraham, Muhammad never goes so far as to reject them completely. Thus, unlike the followers of polytheistic religions, condemned to conversion or death, Jews and Christians remain tolerated by the Muslims. Nevertheless they have to put up with inferior status, evidence of the truth of Islam – this ambivalent attitude, reminiscent of the Christian approach to the Jews – led to the status of *dhimmi* (protected). The *dhimmi* is permitted to practise his religion in return for the payment of a special tax. This law – a true legal and social humiliation thus carries with it certain limitations: banned from riding horseback or carrying weapons, compulsion to wear distinctive clothing, segregation in public places. Even when they are active in economic life, daily restrictions constantly remind them of their inferior status.

Professor Ronald Nettler of Oxford University emphasises that Muslim legislation is broadly unfavourable to the Jews.[47] As *dhimmis* they were subject to a special tax and were compelled to wear a distinctive badge on their garment. Sometimes it was the *ghiyar* in a colour different from their garment that the *dhimmis* had to attach to their shoulder, and at times the *zunnar* or special belt they had to wear. The Abassid Caliph, Haroun al-Rashid, was the first known sovereign to have imposed this law.

In 807 he commanded the Jews to wear a piece of yellow cloth on their clothing, and ordered the destruction of their synagogues.[48]

For all that he was regarded as deceitful and a profiteer, the fact remains however that in Islamic countries the Jew never inspired the same kind of hatred that he was subjected to by the Christians. Overall, he was considered a weak and distrusted creature. It was precisely this image that was to alter with time:

The specifically Christian form of Jew-hatred entered the Muslim world in stages. The first manifestations go back to the Early Middle Ages. The second phase began with the conquest of Constantinople and the Ottoman expansion through Europe, bringing a great number of Orthodox Christians under Muslim rule. Endemic in the newly conquered Greek provinces, the Ottoman authorities were alerted to the charge of ritual murder because of the disturbances that broke out every year at Easter time. It was the first time this kind of anti-Jewish libel surfaced on Islamic soil. However it was not until the nineteenth century that modern antisemitism began to spread in the Muslim world. Stemming from Christian Arab minorities, which of all the Middle Eastern communities, had the closest links with the west, it was actively encouraged by every kind of western emissary, consular and commercial attachés, but also by priests and missionaries.[49]

The Damascus Affair

During the nineteenth century the accusation of ritual murder became the norm throughout the Arab, Greek and Turkish provinces of the empire. The most famous case is most probably the Damascus Affair. In 1840 a Capuchin monk, Father Thomas, mysteriously disappeared one day from the Christian area of this town. Driven by the French Consul, Ratti-Menton, several Franciscan monks attributed his disappearance to the Jewish community and launched proceedings against the leaders, accusing them of ritual murder.[50] Under lengthy torture, some yielded, others converted, and there were some who finally gave false testimony. Astonishingly, the government of Adolphe Thiers sided with the Consul in Damascus. Yet *Le Messager*, a government publication, was responsible for writing that the superstitions of oriental Jews forbade ritual murder. It may be that Thiers believed this, writes Leon Poliakov. What did he know about Judaism? The fact remains that trapped by misrepresentations of his own making, he was eventually obliged to resign. As for the French Consul in Damascus, his government later decorated him. As a result the image of the demonic Jew as a drinker of blood was implanted on Muslim soil.

Although alien to the tradition of Islam it was gradually to take root and end up by being fundamental, as our study will show. There is no doubt that the success of this propaganda is linked with the establishment and development of the State of Israel. Presenting the Jews as satanic creatures was to prove useful to the political and religious elites of the Arab nations – when all was said and done, it provided a credible explanation for the crushing defeats of 1948 and 1967 (how can one hope to fight against a people that has asserted its evil power over the entire world?); at the same time it largely exonerated those same elites from responsibility for their inability to defeat 'little' Israel.

Paradoxically it was at the very time when, after centuries of obscurantism, Europe discovered the virtues of tolerance, that the Arab-Muslim world united for blatantly expedient reasons to appropriate the stereotypes that were hitherto unknown there – the theory of Jewish conspiracy aiming at world domination, ritual murder and deicide. Thus for example when the Pope visited Syria in 2001, President Bashir El Assad referred not to the 'Zionist occupation' but to the Jews, accusing them of having both tortured Christ and plotted against Muhammad.

From the moment it took hold on Islamic soil, entering the mind of the elites and the unconscious of the peoples, antisemitism adapted to the requirements of its new publicists. Whereas the Arab-Islamic lands had hitherto been content to translate the great 'classics' of Western anti-Judaism (from the *Protocols of the Elders of Zion* to *Mein Kampf*, and other French revisionist works) original texts written in Arabic now appeared in response to the special needs of local antisemitism. In his book *The Matzah of Zion*, Moustafa Tlass, the irremovable Syrian minister of defence (1972-2004), goes back to the Damascus Affair, stubbornly asserting against all evidence the culpability of the Jews.

Cover of a work entitled 'Matza and Zion' by the Syrian Minister of Defence, Moustafa Tlass

Going by the issue of the Egyptian satirical weekly, *Rose Al-Yousouf*, published on 24 February 2001, it was to be made into a film. This film, the Egyptian producer explained, would be the Arab response to '*all those Zionist films distributed by the American film industry.*'

It was to be called *The Matzah of Zion*, like Tlass's book or *Harari's List* – the name of the rabbi in Damascus accused of ritual murder – alluding to 'the Zionist propaganda film' *Schindler's List*.

Similarly, some years earlier, when an Arab scholar, representing Saudi Arabia at a United Nations seminar on religious freedom in December 1984, attributed the following statement to the Talmud: '*A Jew who does not drink the blood of a non-Jew once a year is damned for all eternity*'. '*The essence of this Saudi intellectual's contribution to religious tolerance,*' writes Bernard Lewis, reporting the event, '*consisted of giving a detailed account of the famous Damascus trial held in 1840 and confirming the truth of the accusations.*'[51]

More recently during a meeting with President Hosni Mubarak in November 2000, Abraham Foxman, national director of the Anti-Defamation League (ADL), supplied proof of numerous instances of shifts towards antisemitism in the Egyptian press. He referred in particular to an article that appeared shortly before (on 28 October 2000) in the leading Egyptian daily *Al-Ahram*. The contents can be guessed from the title: 'A Jewish *Matza* made from Arab blood'. Drawing on the Damascus Affair of 1840 as evidence, one of its columnists attempted to demonstrate that the Israelis used the blood of Palestinian children to make unleavened bread. Abraham Foxman invited President Mubarak to issue a public condemnation of such an absurd myth, likely to intensify an already heated political situation. President Mubarak did nothing.[52]

The media and its constant reference to the vampire Jew

Today the myth of ritual crime is commonplace in the heart of the Arab-Muslim world. Evidence of this is the endlessly growing number of Islamic sites putting online the *Protocols of the Elders of Zion*, and the by now classic antisemitic study *My Irrelevant Defence, being meditations inside gaol and out on Jewish ritual murder*, published in 1938 in London by Arnold Spencer Leese in editions of the Imperial Fascist League. The way that the myth has become commonplace makes it easier to understand the increasing excesses of the Arab media. Witness the satirical programme shown on Abu Dhabi's television on 17

An actor disguised as Ariel Sharon ordering his soldiers to kill Palestinian children to drink their blood

A mock poster showing Sharon as a satanic rabbi, praising the virtues of *Dra Cola*

November 2001, presenting Prime Minister Ariel Sharon not only as a fearsome lover of human blood, but also as responsible for the death of Dracula, his most dangerous… rival. A further instance supporting this theory is the article published in the Saudi Arab daily *Al-Riyadh*, written by Dr Umayma Ahmed Al-Jalahma of the University of King Feisal of Al-Dammam. In it she states that the Jewish festival of Purim *'consists of certain dangerous customs that will doubtless terrify you'.* And the journalist begins by making her excuses in advance for the horrific content she is about to relay to her readers:

During this festival the Jew must prepare some very special pastries, with a filling that is not only costly and rare, but cannot be bought either on the local or the international market. Nor can this essential ingredient unfortunately be omitted, or replaced by some other preparation to fulfil the same function. For this festival the Jews have to obtain human blood so that their priests can prepare the special Purim pastries. In other words the festival cannot be celebrated as custom requires without the spilling of human blood! Before going into further detail, I should like to confirm that the Jews use human blood to prepare the pastries for their festival – this is a well-established fact, both historically and legally throughout history. This fact constitutes one of the fundamental reasons for the persecution and exile that have been the lot of the Jews in Europe and in Asia in different epochs. This festival (Purim)

begins with a fast on 13 March in memory of the Jewess Esther, who made the vow to fast. It continues during 14 March. During the festival the Jews put on carnival masks and costumes, drink alcohol to excess and wallow in prostitutions and adultery. This festival has become famous among Muslim historians as 'The Festival of the Masks'.

…For this festival the victim has to be a healthy adolescent, a non-Jew it goes without saying, that is to say a Christian or a Muslim. His blood is drawn, then dried to a powder. The priest adds the powder to the dough intended for the pastries; the powder can also be reserved for the following festival. This differs from the Pesach sacrifice (on the subject I shortly intend to write a few lines), when the blood of Christian or Muslim children less than 10 years old has to be used, and the priest can add this blood (to the dough) either before or after it is dried' [53]

The journalist goes on to explain that the blood of the victims is obtained from a barrel stuck with needles, thus permitting the blood to trickle out from it very slowly.

Thus the victim is subjected to appalling torture, a torture that affords the vampire Jews huge delight as they control every detail of the bloodshed with pleasure and enjoyment that are hard to imagine. Following this barbarous spectacle, the Jews put the blood poured into a bottle placed at the bottom (of the barrel spiked with nails) and the Jewish priest raises his co-religionists to the peak of happiness when during the festival they are served with pastries mixed with human blood … There is another way of making blood flow. The victim can have his throat cut, in the same way as a sheep, and the blood is collected into a vessel. Or even by cutting his veins in several places and letting the blood pour from his body. The blood is collected with great care – as I have already pointed out – by the 'rabbi', the Jewish priest who specialises in making these kinds of pastries.

In conclusion the author writes: 'human beings cannot bring themselves even to look at the Jewish pastries, let alone either to produce or eat them'.

'This is the germ that Arafat has' (Sharon as an evil microbe).
Hamed Atz, *Akbar Al Khaleej* (Bahrain), 11 February 2004

Nasser welcoming Arafat to heaven:
'I was also poisoned before you'
Jihad Awartani, *Ad Dustour* (Jordan), 9 November 2004

From now on the myth of the vampire Jew and child murderer crops up in the Arab world at the slightest excuse, as in this humorous letter sent by a certain Gaby Nasr to the very Christian Lebanese daily, *L'Orient-Le Jour,* on 10 October 2002, on the subject of the River Wazanni.[54] Here, as Elisabeth Schemla has pointed out on her daily web *Proche-Orient info*, we find all the old anti-Jewish clichés reappearing, the role of child murderer being handed down to a deservedly demonised Sharon.

Since George Dubya decided to welcome the Baghdadi with the moustache, nearby Ariel with the paunch next door hasn't stopped hunting for lice in his star-spangled banner. Sometimes it's the chatter of the flunkeys about the killer lightning… fired by Rambo at the date-palm paradise; sometimes it's Arafat that he puts on a diet in his Ramallah shed; or then it's the helicopter strafes that he sends against unborn children and nursing babies. The truth of the matter is that the maniac with the kippah is jealous. How he would have loved to be perched on his white chariot, at the head of a fearsome international coalition entrusted with the task of giving a free shave to all those beards in the Middle East. Only that Dubya in the White House, who keeps him as a dog for his bitch, doesn't stop telling him he should put them down.

But go on, typical… Plug one orifice and he'll open up another, this buddy of Sharon's. His latest craze is the Wazzani. Three million wretched cubic metres and it's the 'casus

Mohamed Effat Ismail is the president of the Egyptian section of
FECO (Federation of European Cartoonists' Organization),
11 September 2002

Elie Saliba, *Al Watan* (Qatar), 23 May 2002

*belli'. Dracula makes the haemoglobin spurt, and changes
himself into water!… Would you believe!! […]'*
Speaking of water, we have to point out the persistence
of another *antisemyth* in Arab lands, deriving from the
medieval Christian tradition – of the Jew as poisoner. This
myth, most blatantly expressed during the Middle Ages by
the accusation of poisoning the wells (with germs from the
Black Plague or leprosy), has become increasingly popular in the Middle East today. The Israelis are supposedly
spreading noxious substances (particularly in the form of
sweets distributed to children), polluting of ground water,
releasing gases and other radioactive materials into the air,
not to mention the Aids virus deliberately being spread (as

widely as possible) into the heart of the Arab population.
These allegations, make no mistake about it, are being
given widespread prominence. Yasser Arafat had no qualms
in accusing the Israelis of resorting to using impoverished
uranium against the Arabs; his wife Souha went so far as to
complain to Hillary Clinton about the 'poisoning actions'
taken by Israel.[55]

Finally, let us not forget that the (natural) death of Arafat in a Parisian hospital was also attributed to Israel. Many
– from Arafat's own nephew to Leila Shahid, then PLO representative to the European Union, claimed that he had been
poisoned, a return to the absolutely classic 'antisemyth' of the
Jew as a poisoner.

The Jews and Israel in contemporary Arab cartoons

It is a fact that Arab cartoonists do not work the same way as their European and American counterparts. The cartoon is an art form that requires a minimum of freedom in order to exist. The framework best suited to it is the democratic public arena. Caricature, as we have seen, is the distortion of a face, an image, a given situation in order to create a picture truer than nature. Its intention is to provoke a shocked reaction, an awareness of society. This has not always been easy. In 1834 King Louis-Philippe banned *La Caricature*, a satirical journal founded four years earlier by Charles Philipon[56] and Honoré de Balzac. In the same way, in our own time cartoons are an art form still kept under the strictest supervision in most countries of the world. From distant Asia to the vastness of Africa, by way of the Middle East, cartoonists able to practise their art free of constraint are few and far between. By this we are not claiming that there are no cartoons in Chinese, Congolese or Syrian papers, for example, but that under a dictatorial regime they do not for the most part fulfil the objective theoretically assigned to them – to act as an irritant to the current regime, to jostle those in power, the scoundrels, the hypocrites, the profiteers, to point the finger at the incompetent or the snobbish. The strength of someone like Plantu is to attack, mostly in a funny way, not just Putin or Sharon, but also Jacques Chirac or Lionel Jospin. Quite obviously, it's essential for effective cartoons to be able to turn the tables and make one laugh at oneself.

So following the example of their Russian colleagues under the USSR, the leading Palestinian cartoonists, no matter how talented, hardly dare venture into the field of self-criticism. Do they note injustices? Do they denounce scandalous situations? They rarely do. This calls to mind Michel Kichka's observation: *A cartoonist is not a journalist. He is not obliged to be objective. He may, in fact he must express an opinion. At the time of the Netanyahu and the Barak governments, I hardly ever drew Yasser Arafat. By focusing on Bibi and Barak, I wanted to show that the ball was in our court. I often find it necessary to support, to attack or even to ignore a personality, but I never forget that my function is to criticise the government currently in power.'[57]

Arab cartoonists hardly[58] ever denounce the base acts or the errors of their own governments, or at best very mildly.[59] How many drawings are there covering the fate of the Kurds, the Sudanese, the Saharans, homosexuals in Egypt, not to mention women, and Hindus in Afghanistan obliged by the fundamentalist Taliban to wear some yellow distinctive badge? And obviously, never the least allusion to terrorist attacks on civilians in Israel. These cartoonists do not as a rule sign up to social criticism and humour, the two fundamentals of the cartoonist's art, but to pure indignation. Their drawings are for the most part heavy, serious and moralising. They are essentially weapons in the service of a cause that does not go too deep. There is no place for irony here.

The idea of caricature is to magnify a feature, and exaggerate it to excess so that the reality to which it refers becomes itself more visible, more legible. Now in portraying the Jews as blood-drinkers and Sharon as a predator (vampire, shark, snake etc.), by sketching Israelis in uniforms adorned with

Rasmy (Jordan), *Arabia.com*, 25 June 2001
A rabbi brandishing a *menorah* controls the American beast

the swastika, by plundering the prop room and wheeling out the crucifixion of Jesus and the mediaeval accusation of the blood libel, 'anti-Zionist' cartoonists don't magnify anything, no real features are drawn on – all they do is to dip into the antisemitic myths, condemned and relegated to oblivion everywhere else. Tristan Mendès France and Michael Prazan have drawn attention to this trend: '*The antisemitic themes are repeated ad nauseam – the Jewish conspiracy aimed at world domination; the Jewish poisoner and source of contagious diseases (the most recent example to date being Aids) going right back to the medieval accusation of ritual murder which reappears from time to time. The confusion of Zionism (or what is taken to be Zionism) and Nazism is particularly insidious. The majority of Arab political commentators or cartoonists seem incapable of criticising any aspect of Israeli government policy without dubbing it 'Nazi policy', or of depicting Israeli leaders other than wearing swastikas.*[60]

European constitution
Amjad Rasmi, *Arabnews*, 20 June 2004

Arab cartoons: the need for a scapegoat

The formula is an old-established one: to unite a people, there is nothing better than a good old accusation levelled at the Jews !

To be fair, we mustn't forget the undemocratic character of the countries where these cartoonists live and practise their profession. In this regard, let's not forget that Naji Al-Ali, the father of Palestinian cartoonists, and one of the best known in the Arab world, was gunned down in the heart of London on 22 July 1987, probably by a PLO commando for having been too explicit about the personality of Yasser Arafat.[61] This surely explains why the most famous Palestinian cartoonist, Omayya Joha, acknowledges that he never tackles the leader of the Palestinian Authority: '*I have too much respect for him – he is the President.*'[62]

By cutting themselves off from the real world – which they are obliged to portray to their own people in a distorted way, by means of images based on myths – the Arab cartoonists betray their mission. Given that a cartoonist will denounce Israel's politics, even in an outrageous and excessive manner, for that is part of his brief, it is on the other hand contrary to his own ethics and professional code to make his pencil lie. Now the image that he sketches unrelentingly of Israelis and Jews is nothing but lies and fantasy.

Debarred from comment on his preferred subject (social debate and internal politics), the Arab-Muslim newspaper cartoonist is for the most part reduced to firing his shafts at the outside world with a violence, aggression and bad faith corresponding to his own frustration. Is he gagged and fettered? Is the world evil and unjust? Are people's living conditions wretched? The fault lies with others: the West, the Crusades, the freemasons, and above all: the Americans and the Jews – the two latter, it has to be said, unrecognisably portrayed as remote from any reality, too monstrous, too cruel to be… credible. Except for the Arab masses whose only knowledge of the afore-mentioned Americans and Jews stems from what has long been dinned into them day after day and year after year by their own press. The idea is quite simple: all the misfortunes of the Arab world are the fault of the Jews and/or the crusaders. The Arab world is innocent by nature, victim by definition. This vision is clearly expressed in the way the Arabic cartoonists see the Darfur ethnic cleansing. It is either presented as a pure fiction, or as a propaganda tool used against the Arab world.

The Arab world is innocent by nature: proof by Darfur

After Afghanistan and Iraq, It's Sudan's Turn for UN Security Council Mayhem
Amjad Rasmi, Arab News, 3 April 2005

The Sudanese civil war in Darfur
Hamed, Alittihad, 27 September 2004

The US, the UN and the Sudan
Mustafa Rahmeh, Alittihad, 27 September 2004

Amjad Rasmi

The Arab League:
1. Was dealt a great blow when it could not help Palestinians stay in their homeland.
2. Was dealt a greater blow when it failed to prevent the US-UK invasion of Iraq.
3. The fatal blow will be in its inability to prevent a looming US-UK invasion of a third Arab state, Sudan, using the Darfur excuse.
Amjad Rasmi, Arab News, 8 August 2004

– Why do you care to interfere in Darfur anyway?
– I want to make sure that you'll continue the hostility among each other.
Mustafa Rahmeh, Alittihad, 30 July 2004

The Sudan Hostage, about to be beheaded by Britain, the US, and the UN sanctions
Rabei, *Al-Riyadh* (Saudi Arabia), 30 July 2004

Kofi Annan about to impose US-UK-induced sanctions
on Sudan
Rabei, Al-Riyadh, 28 September 2004.

Western aid to Darfur
Mustafa Rahmeh, Alittihad, 12 August 2004

The US to Sudan: 'You've committed genocide in Darfur.'
Israeli Prime Minister Sharon: 'Ha Ha Ha.'
Tulba, Al-Ahram, 28 July 2004

Mustafa Rahmeh, *Alittihad*, 9 August 2004

The US to Sudanese President El-Bashir: 'This [Darfur crisis] is to reward you for your cooperation in signing the peace agreement with the Southern Sudanese in Kenya.'
Hamed Ata, Al-Khaleej, 11 August 2004

Cartoon by Gomaa
Al-Ahram weekly, 22–28 July 2004

Recurring features of Arab and Soviet antisemitism

Until fairly recently the Jews were of minor interest to the Muslims, but as we have seen, since the 1980s they have been appearing as the principal menace hanging over the world and over Islam. Their portrayal by the Koran as cowardly and ridiculous, mean schemers and in its wake in the pre-1967 Arab press, has shifted to a new representation as devilish conspirators aiming at nothing less than world domination. To go by today's Arab press, they are the imperialists, manipulating the United States, or Turkey,[63] as if those countries were mere puppets at their beck and call.

Whereas Arab antisemitism gained a fresh impetus from the beginning of the 1980s onwards, it actually pre-dates this period. The cartoons reproduced below, published in the Arab press just before the Six Day War, depict the Israelis as vile, degenerate and debased beings. The Jew is now portrayed as sub-human – he is undoubtedly devilish, but also undersized, ugly and cowardly, leading to the assumption that his planned elimination, explicitly and unambiguously proclaimed by cartoonists, will hardly be much effort for the Arab nation to achieve.

In their triumphalism the pre-1967 Arab cartoons present an image of Jews that has nothing in common with those appearing in Soviet newspapers at the same period. Here the Jew is not portrayed as 'dominating', 'Nazi' or 'money-grubbing', in the particular manner favoured by

كيف نستعمـــل نجمة اسرائيل ..

'How to use the Star of David'
Al Manar (Iraq), 8 June 1967

« المعركة المقدسة »

'The Holy War'
Al Goumhourya, 8 June 1967

the cartoonists of the Communist bloc. Israelis are shown as vile creatures sometimes with Semitic features, sometimes demonic, that could easily be driven into the sea.[64]

In Soviet cartoons from the same period the 'Zionist' is portrayed sometimes as a capitalist, sometimes a Nazi, in the service of American imperialism. Here it is no more a matter of the Israelis dictating their policies to the United States – on the contrary, it is the Americans who are in the lead and manipulate their 'people' in the Middle East.

The eight Arab states will destroy Israel.
'The guns of eight countries'
Al-Djarida, Lebanon, 3 May 1967

Three examples of Soviet antisemitic cartoons:

'Israel and the Nazis, one and the same',
Sovietskaya Moldaa, 22 January 1972

'The leader and his lackey'
Izvestia, 24 March 1970

The Zionist Jew (written on his waistcoat)
is shown here as a vile being, greedy for
money and relishing conspiracy.
Gudak, 4 August 1973

Chapter 3

Arab cartoons since 2000

Today the pattern has reversed. From being weak, the Jew is shown as strong. The dwarf has been transformed into a giant. David has turned into Goliath. How else can the crushing defeat of 1967 be accounted for than by promoting the idea of the evil Jew, endowed with supernatural powers? 'Attributing an Arab defeat not to Israeli know-how (thus contradicting the stereotypical image of the fearful, cowardly Jew) but to some mysterious weapon that Israel obtained by Satanic means, provides a plausible rationalisation that the public can relate to. The shame and humiliation are thereby rendered more tolerable while searching for a way of taking revenge.' [65]

From now on the portrayal of the Jew as a demonic, powerful and cruel being becomes the only possible one. It transcends the contingencies and vagaries of politics in general and proceeds beyond them to specific periods in history. The Jew is evil in Syria, in Palestine, and even in Jordan and Egypt, despite the two latter countries' peace treaty with Israel. It should indeed be stressed that far from diminishing in virulence with the signing of the Oslo Peace Process by Rabin, Peres and Arafat, the anti-Israeli and antisemitic imagery in the Arab press has persisted and intensified since the second *intifada*. Egypt resumed diplomatic relations with Israel in 1978, and yet it is one of the worst sources of antisemitic images. Prior to 'Sharon the butcher', there were other 'butchers' targeted by the Egyptian cartoonists – none other than Nobel Prize winners Rabin and Peres. State of war or peace talks, Sharon or Rabin, Oslo or no Oslo, *intifada* or no *intifada,* Israelis remain the enemy, not only of Egypt, Syria or Palestine but of humankind in general. And anything goes, however shameful, to malign and attack them.

The illustrations that follow give some idea of the means employed. They are arranged according to subject:

1. Israeli=Judaism=vermin and demonic creature.
2. Israel subjects Palestine to the same martyrdom the Jews inflicted on Jesus.
3. The Jew/Israeli is an animal. He's a predator, a venomous snake, squalid rat, stinking hyena, a spider spinning a web.
4. The Jews/Israelis dominate the world. They control the United States.
5. Israel's domination is underpinned by money.
6. The Jews/Israelis are blood lovers and Sharon is a vampire.
7. Palestinian babies and children are the prime targets of the Jew/Israeli.
8. Sharon is the absolute monster and Olmert is his devoted successor.
9. The Jew/Israeli is a liar. The 'Peace Process' is just an Israeli plot to destroy the Arab world. Israel is responsible for all the misfortunes of the Arab world. Israel is behind the Lebanon crisis and the Iraq war.
10. The Israelis are worse than the Nazis – who have been unjustly accused. The Zionists make use of the Shoah, whereas the Palestinians are in fact the victims of a real Holocaust.
11. The Jew/Israeli is a satanic creature that must be eliminated for the salvation of humanity.

What is an antisemitic cartoon?

An antisemitic cartoon is certainly not a drawing that just mocks, criticises or even denounces Israel as such. Anti-Zionism is still an opinion, not an offence. And, independently even of this remark and/or question, how not to accept that the principle of caricature is to criticise and, more than often, to play on weak points, to attack where it will hurt the most! So are cartoons cruel? Of course they are. As we have already said, to get the message across, a cartoonist will outrageously inflate the tiniest defect, by taking it to extremes. To expose, to amplify, to exaggerate is the very essence of his function. The key word of caricature is 'exaggeration', not 'invention'. A good caricature is based on truthfulness, not mythology. So, what is a good cartoon? It is a work that rests on… truth. Of course the cartoonist's works may be in bad taste and/or bad faith but provided he starts out from a particular truth, he is doing his job.

What does this mean? Emphatically that any cartoon attributing to the Israeli 'racial' features (*Stürmer*-like Jew), falsified history (deicide), untrue practice (ritual murder), invented rituals (infanticide), scurrilous accusations (genocide) is essentially antisemitic. There is not one ounce of truth in the infanticide accusation: Judaism does not ask Jews or Israelis to kill Muslim or Christian children in order to make matzos! Not to mention, that the Jews have nothing to do with Satanism and… Danish cartoons. Unfortunately, 90 per cent of the cartoons found in the Arab press relating to the Israeli–Palestinian conflict are based on antisemitic mythology.

Judaism behind the Danish cartoon affair!
Elie Saliba, *Al Watan* (Qatar), 19 February 2006

'Here's to peace!'
The image takes us back to the twelfth century and the notion of ritual murder. *Al Ahram* (Egypt), 21 April 2001

Two emblematic examples of what an antisemitic cartoon is

Cartoons by subject

1. The Jew as enemy of humanity *(=demonism)*

Historians, professors of racial studies and sociologists are all agreed in maintaining that in its long history the human race has never known a race with so many vile and despicable characteristics as the Jewish race. The Jews possess a characteristic that distinguishes them from others whenever they have settled in a particular place and feel comfortable there, they have transformed that place into a den of evil, of corruption, of incitement to divisiveness and to an increase in conflict … There is no difference, as maintained by some, between yesterday's Jew and the Jew of today, or between Jewish identity and Israeli identity. Indeed, as a state, Israel is the recipient of all the Jews in the world. Zionism is the political and colonial aspect of the Jewish religion.

(Hassan Soueïlem, reserve general, in *October*, Egyptian major circulation weekly, 3 December 2000)

Stavro Jabra, Lebanon, *Daily Star*, 4 April 2002.
This cartoon typifies the Arab form of antisemitism. Following the classic tradition of antisemitism, the cartoonist – a Lebanese Christian – here attacks the Talmud, i.e. the commentaries on the Bible. Here it is the Talmud – once burned in Paris – that triggers the bullet from the assassin's rifle. Here Judaism, and not Zionism, is denounced.

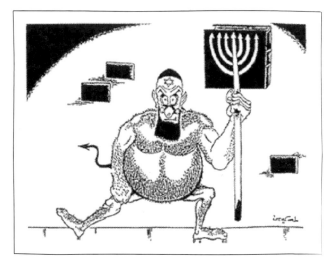

Ali Farazat, *Al Watan* (Kuwait), 10 June 2006

Egypt, 4 March 1992

'The real Bible'. The Talmud may be the prime target, but the Bible isn't spared either.

Al-Hayat al-Jadida, organ of the Palestinian Authority,
28 December 1999, namely long before the second intifada.
The old man's djellabah reads *'The twentieth century'*, the young man's t-shirt
'The twenty-first century', and above the Jew runs the inscription 'The disease of the century'.
The cartoon implies that the Jew is not a human being but a despicable condition.

Daily Star, Beirut, 8 September 2001, 3 days before 11 September.
The Lebanese Stavro Jabra identifies the true cause of the evils of the world – arrogance and Jewish racism.

Siamak Saharkhiz (Iran)

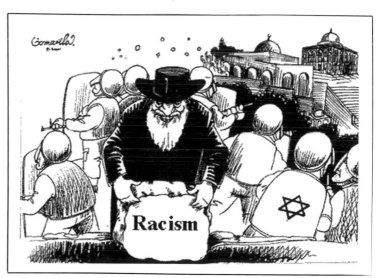

Gomaa Farhat, *Al Ahram* Weekly Online, 2–8 August 2001.
Al Ahram is the principal Egyptian quasi-governmental daily newspaper.
Here Gomaa is attacking Judaism: a rabbi incites racism with one of the
stone tablets of the Law.

خطة الأنسحاب !

Emad Hajjaj, *Alquds Alarabi*, 29 October 2004
Sharon drawing his disengagement plan

Tallil Abdel Latef (Morocco), *Arabcartoon*,
5 July 2006

The Torah is here clearly used as a weapon.
The basis of Judaism is world domination.
Al-Istiqlal (Palestine), 3 April 2001

2. The Jews kill Palestine just as they killed Christ (=deicide)

It is the same mentality that made them betray and torture Jesus Christ and similarly attempt to betray the Prophet Muhammad, that makes them try to kill all divine principles of faith.

(President Bashar el-Assad to Pope John Paul II, Damascus, 5 May 2001, according the official SANA news agency)

Boukhari, *Arabia.com*, 7 April 2002.
In the Middle Ages the chief indictment levelled against the Jews was that of deicide. Although challenged since Vatican II, it is nevertheless still at the core of Palestinian propaganda. The idea is to turn Jesus the Jew into the first Palestinian victim of... the Jews.

Al Intifada, 14 December 2000.

At the foot of the Cross a Jewish trio with stereotypical features – simian mouth and jaw and hooked nose – with the blood of 'Palestine', the innocent victim, dripping down on them. The cartoonist is giving a nod and a wink towards the Christians, as if to say: 'Here you are, the re-run of the Passion of Christ'.

Omayya Joha, *Arabcartoon, 15 March*

43

Jalal Al-Rifai, *Ad Dustour*, 12 July 2004.
Crucified twice in about 2,000 years, once on the Cross,
again on the Greed Wall.

Baha Boukhari (Palestine), *Arabia.com*, 5 May 2002

Stavro Jabra, *Daily Star*, 4 April 2002.
Judging by these two cartoons, Jesus is once again the intended victim of the Jews. The fact that Bethlehem was Jewish at the time of Jesus and predominantly Muslim today is of no significance. The point is to address their image of the Western Christian.

Stavro, Lebanon, *Daily Star*, 10 April 2002
Those who crucified the Prophet have crucified my
people tonight

Nasser Al-Ja'nfari, *Al Quds*, 25 December 2002
Bethlehem crucified by the occupation

Boukhari, *Arabia.com*, 'Curfew', 1 December 2002.
By presenting Jesus as a Palestinian, the cartoonists kill two birds with one stone: besides harping on the notion of the 'deicide people',
they manage to overlook the fact that in the time of Herod and Pontius Pilate there were no Palestinian Arabs in Judea.

One of the very first portrayals of Palestine crucified
(1983?), the work of the father of Palestinian cartoonists,
Naji Al-Ali,
Al-Istiqal (Palestine), 1 June 2001

Stavro Jabra, 29 February 2004

3. Cartoons using animal forms (=zoomorphism)

Consult history and it teaches us that the Jews of yesterday are an evil legacy, while those of today are even worse – ungrateful towards their benefactors, worshippers of the Golden Calf, prophet murderers, word-twisters, deniers of divine utterances, opponents of authority, pilgrims of ruin, scum of humanity. Despised and banished by God, who has turned them into apes, pigs and idol-worshippers that have turned aside from the true path. Such are the Jews: a succession of constant injustices, obstinacy, hypocrisy, treason and depravity. They sow the seeds of depravity on earth, and God does not like depravity. They set up networks and cells of oppression, of resentment, of hypocrisy and vileness… The time is near when the Muslims will combat and kill them, when the Jew will have to hide behind a rock or a tree, and, and the rock or the tree will say to the Muslim, 'You, Muslim, you, God's slave, there is a Jew hiding behind me, step forward and kill him.'

(Extracts from a sermon broadcast live from Mecca on Radio Orient, on 27 October, 2000, and reprinted in *l'Arche* (monthly publication of French Jewry), September 2001, p.67).

Stavro Jabra (Lebanon), *Daily Star*, 23 October 2000
Barak interrupting the peace process

Baha Boukhari (Palestine), *Arabia.com*, 8 April 2002

47

In the manner of Nazi cartoons and propaganda, the Arab cartoonists rely on presenting the Jew in bestial form. The Jews are noxious, inhuman and harmful creatures. They constitute a menace not only to Palestine and the Arab world, but also to the whole of mankind.

Stavro, *La Revue du Liban*, 8 December 2001

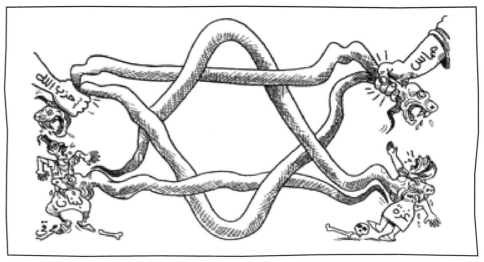

Abdala Mahraqy, *Akhbar Al-Khaleej* (Bahrain), 14 July 2006

الأنتخابات الأسرائيلية !

www.mahjoob.com

Emad Hajjaj, *Ad Dustour* (Jordan), 3 February 2001, posted on www.mahjoob.com
Barak and Sharon, the two-headed monster

Cartoon reproduced by the ADL, 22 October 2000

Khaldoun Gharaybeh, *Al-Ra'i* (Jordan), 29 June 2006

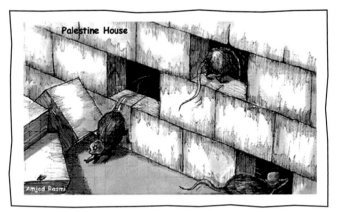

Amjad Rasmi, *Arab News* (Saudi Arabia), n.d.
This cartoon may be inspired by a scene from the Nazi film *Jew Suess*, in which Jews are depicted as vermin to be eradicated by mass extermination.

Husam Daghlas (Jordan), reproduced by *Arabcartoon*, fourth week of July 2006.

4. The Jews as 'world dominators' (=*Protocols of the Elders of Zion*)

Zionism ... has fabricated myths on the subject of the Nazi Holocaust suffered by the Jews, and inflated them to astronomic proportions ... Israel and the Zionist organisations have two objectives: firstly, to obtain money from Germany and from European states and bodies; and then to employ the legend of the Holocaust as a sword of Damocles over the heads of those who oppose Zionism, in order to accuse them of antisemitism.
(Mohammed Kheir Al-Wadi, editor in chief of the Syrian official daily, *Teshreen*, 31 January 2000)

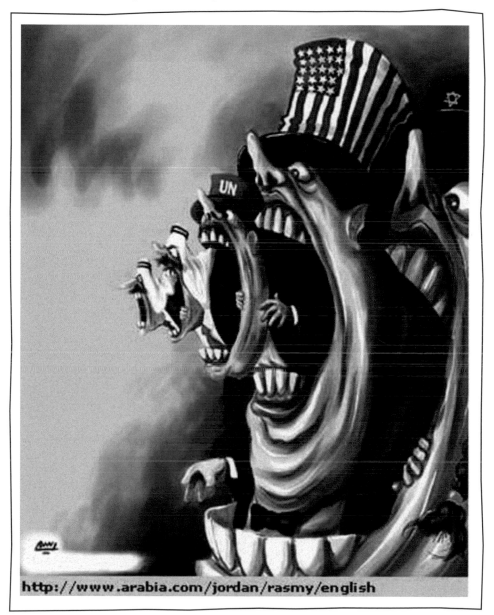

http://www.arabia.com/jordan/rasmy/english

Rasmy, *Arabia.com*, 17 October 2001
Israel, that dominates the US, that dominates UNO, that dominates the Arab world...

Omayya Joha
Clinton the Barak puppet

The theme of the Jew as world dominator is standard in the Arab press. For the Arab cartoonists, as for their Nazi and Soviet predecessors, there is no doubt whatever that the Jews are in direct control of the world, via the United States, a puppet state serving the sole interests of the Jews.

Omayya, Alhayat Aljadeeda, 1 March 2003
World puppeteers: Bush in control of the UN and Arab rulers, and Sharon in control of everybody

الشرعية الدولية

Azad Alean, *Al-Ghad* (Jordan), reproduced by *Arabcartoon*, 4 July 2006

Easen Alkalel, *Al-Watan* (Oman) 20 May 2004
The Jew is playing the American 'Governing Council' like a puppet on a
string. The American Government Council is doing the same to the Iraqi
'Governing Council'

Hamed Ata, *Al Ittihad* (UAE), 3 June 2004
The only solution for Israelis to agree to live with the Palestinians: the establishment of One World
Government that rules over all countries of the world and to be called THE UNITED STATES OF ISRAEL

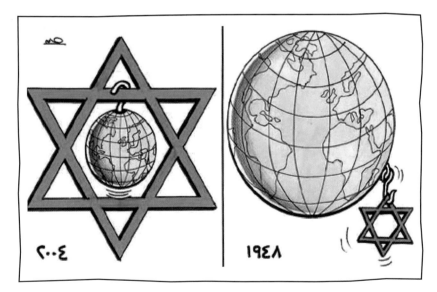

Hamed Ata, *Al Ittihad* (UAE), 15 January 2004
Israel between 1948 (right) and 2004 (left)

Baha Boukhari (Palestine), *Arabia.com*, 17 April 2002

F. Gomaa, *Al Ahram Online* (Egypt), 31 January 6th February 2002

Zaki Shaqfeh, *Al-Ra'i* (Jordan), 16 June 2004
Israel in control of the World System

Hamed Ata, *Al Ittihad* (UAE), 25 November 2002
*'I've also got some papers proving that the whole world belongs to me.
As well as Palestine. That's also mine. Mine and no one else's.*

Zaki Shaqfeh, *Al-Ra'i* (Jordan), 4 June 2004
The US-dominated UN Security Council and the double-standard policy of dealing
with Arabs and Israelis

Jalal Al-Rifai, *Ad Dustour* (Jordan), 6 July 2004
Sharon, Bush and Blair: the Axis of Peace and Democracy

5. The 'antisemyth' of the Jew as a corruptor

Exactly what is it that the Jews want? Read the ninth Protocol of the Elders of Zion … The ultimate aim of the freemasons is to destroy the world and rebuild it according to Zionist policies … in such a way that the Jews can control the world … and destroy its religions … The Jew Karl Marx, with his communism and his Marxism has effectively destroyed the Church in Eastern Europe.
(Mustafa Mahmoud, *Al Ahram*, Cairo, 23 June 2001)

Israel's intention in commemorating the Holocaust is to impose a feeling of culpability onto these countries in order to continue to extort millions of dollars from them.
(Adb Al Azim, *Al Goumhourya*, 22 February 2000)

Bendib (United States), *iview.com*, n.d.

Teshreen (Syria), 18 January 2001

Abdala Mahragy, *Akhbar Al Khaleej* (Bahrain), 10 June 2002
Jew on the right: *'Repeat after me – ''I hate the Arabs!''*
The American repeats: *''I hate the Arabs! I hate the Arabs! I hate the Arabs!''*

Kahil (Lebanon), *Asharq al Awsat* (London-based Saudi affiliated publication), 30 August 2001
Durban Conference on Racism: Israel makes the Americans quit the conference,
against the will of Colin Powell

Khalil Bendib, *iview.com*, n.d.
Al Gore and Joe Lieberman in the clutches of the Jewish lobby

American Muslims made history in 2000 presidential elections when they voted en bloc for George Bush. The American Muslim Political Coordinating Council Political Action Committee (AMPCC-PAC), a coalition of four major American Muslim organisations, only two weeks before the election announced its endorsement of George W. Bush for president, citing his outreach to the Muslim community and his stand on the issue of secret evidence. In a post-election survey of American Muslim voters conducted by the Washington, DC-based Council on American–Islamic Relations (CAIR), one of the nation's largest grassroots Muslim advocacy and civil rights groups, nearly three-quarters of respondents indicated that they had voted for Texas Governor Bush. Of these, 85 per cent noted that the endorsement of Bush by the American Muslim Political Coordinating Committee Political Action Committee (AMPCC-PAC) was a factor in their vote. In this survey of 1,774 voters, 72 per cent of Muslim respondents said they voted for Bush and only 8 per cent favoured Vice President Al Gore. Muslims, therefore, became the only bloc vote for Bush (http://ampolitics.ghazali.net/index.html). According to the Pew research centre (6th December 2004), the Jews did vote for Gore by 79 per cent and Kerry by 75 per cent.

Amjad Rasmi, *Arab News* (Saudi Arabia), 27 July 2004
Again, the Arab lobbies fear a Democrat victory

لاتنتظروا.. غيري

Baha Boukhari, *Al-Ayyam* (Jordan), 25 July 2004

Mohammad Al Rayies, *Arab News* (Saudi Arabia), 2 March 2004
John Kerry, courting US Jewish votes

6. The Jew as a vampire (=blood libel)

Dennis Ross delights in behaving like Shylock, taking pleasure in knowing that he will be able to cut away three per cent of his victim's flesh. (The) biased mediator (is part of) the oppressive Zionist racist apparatus…
(Fatah bulletin, reproduced in the Palestinian Authority's official newspaper, *Al Hayat al Jadida*, 17 September 1998)

This brings us to the nub of our thesis. The Arab cartoonists revive the *antisemyth* of the Jew as a vampire in a heightened form. While the Turks are desperately stealing Arab water, and the Americans their oil, the Jew is after their blood. The Israeli requires fresh blood, especially that of Palestinian children. This image, legacy of another age, is central to contemporary Arab-Muslim cartoons.

The knight of the night, Shaul Mofaz newly appointed Minister of Defence, calling for a terror campaign against Nablus, *Arabia.com*, 2002

Al Bawaba (Jordan and London), 23 November 2000
Sharon wants his share of Muslim blood

Jalal Al-Rifui, *Ad Dustour* (Jordan), 8 March 2006

Omayya Joha, *Al-Hayat al-Jadida*, 9 March 2003
The Zionist Israeli Defence Minister, Shaul Mofaz, and his medals:
Palestinian blood and body parts

Al Ahram (Egypt), 21 April 2001
'Here's to peace!'
The image takes us back to the twelfth century and the notion of ritual murder.
Al Ahram is the daily newspaper of reference of the Arab world. Its circulation is roughly 900,000.

Omayya Joha, *Arabia.com*
The three awards landed by Israel for the massacres at
Deir Yassin, Sabra and Shatilah, and Cana (Lebanon), n.d.

Al-Hayat al-Jadida, 3 September 2001
Collusion between Israel, the United States and the Arab world. *'Your health!'*
(seated on the Arab betrayal)

Amin Merikhi, *Irancartoon*, 2003

Al-Jafari (Jordan), *Arabia.com*, 5 September 2001

Stavro (Lebanon), *Arabia.com*, 13 May 2001

Reza Rezghian (Iran), 2002

Al-Hayat al-Jadida (Jordan), 29 June 2001

Jalal Al-Rifai, *Ad Dustour* (Jordan), 29 June 2006

7. The Jew as child-murderer (=ritual murder)

*The bestial requirement to
knead the matzo Passover
dough with the blood of
gentiles [according to this
translation] occur in the
reports of the Palestinian
police: numerous cases are
recorded in which following
their disappearance, the
bodies of Palestinian
children were discovered in
pieces, without a single drop
of blood remaining. The
most rational explanation
[sic] is that the blood was
removed for use in the
kneading of the dough
prepared by extremist Jews
for making matzos …
In order to put into practice
what is written in the
Talmud, an observant Jew
who keeps the holy decrees is
not entitled to live in any of
the cities sacred to the Jews
(Jerusalem, Hebron, Safed,
Tiberias) unless he has
consumed one of these blood
matzos.'*
(Adel Hamouda,
Al Ahram,
28 October 2000)

www.omayya.com

Omayya (Palestine) In *www.omayya.com*, 28 October 2000
Barak the child murderer protected by the United States

67

Even stronger than the 'antisemyth' of the blood-drinking Jew, is the accusation of ritual murder displayed in the antisemitic nature of contemporary Arab cartoons.

Arab and/or Palestinian cartoonists depict the Israeli predominantly targeting children. It is no coincidence that this particular theme is exploited to excess – in portraying victims exclusively in the guise of children or babies, the intention of the Arab-Muslim propagandists is to make the Palestinians into epitomes of an ill-treated people. However, beyond the daily tragedies endured by the Palestinian people, nothing is further from the truth. The Israeli–Arab conflict has resulted in nearly 4,700 Palestinian victims, but Israelis as well, from the first intifada (1987) to the second (2003). Over the same period of time two million Sudanese, three million Africans from the Great Lakes, 200,000 Bosnians, 150,000 Algerians and 200,000 Chechens have died. Moreover, the fact that the overwhelming majority of Palestinian victims were adults, for the most combatants, and that the Israeli victims included numerous children is never mentioned. The issue is to present the Israelis as the worst executioners in the history of mankind; hence precisely the constant allusions to Nazism. Presenting the conflict as a 'massacre of the innocents' amounts to elevating the Palestinian drama to the level of the Shoah, if not the Gospels (Herod). What better way of affecting public opinion, Arab as well as Western? This explains why ritual child murder, myth of Christian origin, is the favoured strategy circulated and broadcast today. Not without adverse effect. For in fact all it does is to drive some Israelis to utter hatred, an adversary decidedly unlike others. The dramatic intensity and repeated allusion to genocide of these cartoons constitute veritable incitements to murder.

'Nazi bread', Al-Rai Al-Aam (Kuwait), 5 April 1988
The allusion here is two-fold: to the Shoah (crematorium oven) but also to the ritual crime: a Jew (wearing a kipah) making matzo

Omayya (Palestine), Arabia.com, 20 August 2001
'Did he carry a stone?'

Akhbar Elyom (Egypt), 2 December 2000
The Man in the Moon, comic strip made for children during
Ramadan

Omayya (Palestine), *Alraya* (Qatar),
21 June 2006

Tareq Bahar, *Akhbar Al-Khaleej* (Bahrain), 14 July 2006

Baha Boukhari (Palestine), *Al Ayyam* (Jordan), 23 June 2002

Al-Ja'afari (Jordan), *Arabia.com*, 22 May 2001

Omayya (Palestine), *Arabia.com*
'Who did commit the Jenin massacres?'
above: *'Shadows are the only threat to Israel'*, 11 April 2002

Omayya (Palestine), *Arabia.com*, 23 December 2002
Children from Palestine and Iraq

Elie Saliba, *Al-Watan* (Qatar), 17 March 2002 (source: ADL)
It is a Jew, not an Israeli soldier, that is shown murdering the young
Palestinian

Akhbar Al-Khaleej (Bahrain), 6 June 2002 (source : ADL)

Teshreen (Syria), 21 April 2001
Israeli soldiers posing with the corpse of a Palestinian child

8. Sharon as the absolute murderer…

What is the secret behind America's fear of Arafat? What is the secret behind the great powers' leaders' refusal of the American request? … The simple answer is that we think that America is entirely Israel, or that the administration, President Bush, and the Congress are all personally Sharon. They think with his mind and act in the same criminal way.'

'The European countries, Japan, and Canada do not want to go down the American path. Out of self-respect, the leaders of the large industrialized countries do not want to be Sharon … except for Tony Blair, the prime minister of Britain, the former superpower that goes eyeless.'
(Editorial of Egyptian newspaper Al-Akhbar, 'No one would support America if the events of 11 September recurred', 1 July 2002)

I might have accepted the position of many rabbis in the world [who criticised the film] if they had expressed any kind of pain over the suffering of the Palestinians in their struggle against the murderer Ariel Sharon. In the Gospel according to Matthew, the high priest Caiaphas tells the Roman governor Pilate: 'Kill him and his blood will be upon us and upon our children' … I think that Sharon is another Caiaphas and that he – not Mel Gibson – should be condemned.

(Columnist Jihad Al-Khazen, former editor of the London-based Arabic daily Al-Hayat, Al-Hayat (London), 3 March 2004)

Al Ahram (Egypt), 3 August 2002 (source: ADL)
Behind Sharon we read 'Gaza'

Ali Melhem Ali, *Al-Kifah Alarabi* (Lebanon), 21 October 2002
Sharon's solution to the demographic problem

73

إنتخبوا شارون !!

Emad Hajjaj, *mahjoob.com* and *Arabia.com*, 26 January 2003

Wafd (Egypt), 11 May 2001

Al-Watan (Qatar), 19 July 2002

Al Haqiqa (Egypt), 5 May 2001

Sharon in Gaza
Mohammad Al Rayies, *Arab News* (Saudi Arabia), 7 July 2004

Mustafa Rahmeh, *Al Ittihad* (UAE), 22 Januray 2004
His medal and favourite bird

Sharon, the butcher, during his present raid on Gaza
Nagi, *Al-Ahram* (Egypt), 12 May 2004

Sharon protected by the US veto on a UNSC resolution to stop Israeli atrocities and war crimes in northern Gaza Strip
Omayya (Palestine), *Al Hayat Al Jadedah*, 7 October 2004

Amigo (Jordan), Mahjoob.com, 27 January 2004

Samer, *Yemen Time*, 10 May 2004

Sharon and the Palestinian Blood
Hamed Ata, *Akhbar Al-Khaleej* (Bahrain), 19 April 2004

Sharon, the butcher
Hussain, *Al-Ahram* (Egypt), 26 April 2004

Zaid in the official site of the Palestinian Authority press centre,
3 September 2003

Zaid in the official site of the Palestinian Authority press centre, 2001

Omayya, *Al Hayat Al Jadedah*, 9 December 2002
Sharon, the butcher of Jenin at Gaza, and Buraij

Al Jaafari, *Arabia.com*, 26 November 2001
Peres: *'Mr Sharon is not available. He's on the line to the school at Khan Younis'*

The Prime Minister drinks from a cup which looks like the Grail.
'Palestinian Children's Blood' is written on the cup.
Elie Saliba, *Al Watan* (Qatar), 24 July 2002

Omayya (Palestine), *www.omayya.com,* the artist's own site

Bendib, *iviews,* n.d.

Tareq Abu Zeid, *Hebron Times*, Palestine
Right to left:
1. 'Sharon eating the flesh of our children'
2. 'Here's my bottle. The martyr is...'
3. 'They shelled him to make sure it will not explode'
Down: 'They're eating our children, especially their leader'.

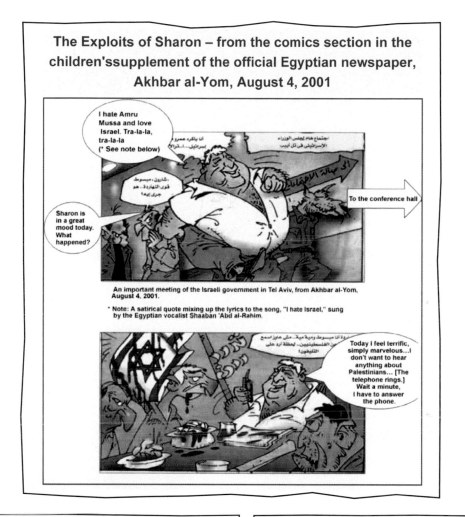

The Exploits of Sharon – from the comics section in the children'ssupplement of the official Egyptian newspaper, Akhbar al-Yom, August 4, 2001

An important meeting of the Israeli government in Tel Aviv, from Akhbar al-Yom, August 4, 2001.

* Note: A satirical quote mixing up the lyrics to the song, "I hate Israel," sung by the Egyptian vocalist Shaaban 'Abd al-Rahim.

Olmert and Peretz as the new bloodthirsty monsters!

Abdala Mahraqy, *Akhbar Al-Khaleej* (Bahrain), 10 June 2006

Gomaa Farahat, *Al Ahram* (Egypt), 30 June 2006

Why do these people hate us? Olmert butchering Palestinians in Gaza unstopped by Bush: Israel has the right to defend itself!
Jala Al-Rifai, *Ad Dustour* (Jordan), 13 June 2006

Emad Hajaj, *Al Quds* (London), 22 June 2006

Abdollah Derkaoui, *Assahra Al-Maghribia* (Morocco),
29 June 2006

Akram Raslan, *Al-Yom* (Saudi Arabia), 29 June 2006

Alaq Allaqeta, *Al Madina* (Saudi Arabia), 11 July 2006

Jalal Al-Rifai, *Ad Dustour* (Jordan), 8 July 2006

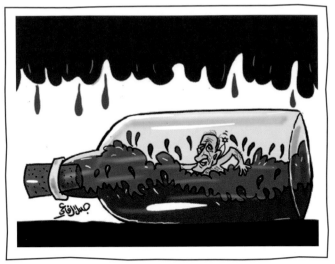

Jalal Al-Rifai, *Ad Dustour* (Jordan), 15 July 2006

Hbeeb Hadad, *Al Hayat* (London), 2 August 2006

Jalal Al-Rifai, *Ad Dustour* (Jordan), 31 July 2006

9. Israel is the (real) Nazi state ('Palestinian holocaust')

Widespread lies assert that Jews were allegedly killed here or there. And, of course, there are just lies without foundation. No Chelmno, no Dachau, no Auschwitz! These were simply disinfection centres… They've always presented themselves as victims and have created a Centre of Heroism and Holocaust. What heroism? What holocaust? Heroism is the heroism of our nation. The holocaust has been committed against our nation…
(Issam Sissalem, staff at the University of Gaza, speaking on Palestinian television, 29 November, 2000)

Long before Sharon came to power, the theme of the Israeli as a Nazi appeared in Arab cartoons everywhere. According to these, all Zionists from Barak to Sharon, by way of Peres, drew their inspiration from Nazi methods. The paradox is glaringly obvious when one remembers, first, the Arab sympathies for the Nazi cause during the Second World War, and then the support – seldom denounced – given by numerous Arab intellectuals to denial theory. According to this perspective the 'Zionist crimes' appear far worse than 'exaggerated Nazi crimes'.

Derkaoui Abdellah (Morocco) made for the Iranian Holocaust competition, 1 June 2006

Emad Hajjaj, *Al-Quds Al-Arabi* (London),
7 August 2006

Stavro Jabra, *Daily Star* (Lebanon), 3 April 2002

Kahil, *Arab News* (London and Saudi Arabia), 10 April 2002

Teshreen (Syria), 15 April 1993
'The Security Council is investigating the case of Palestinian genocide.'
Long list: Israeli crimes
Short list: Nazi crimes

Peres Threatens to Bomb Beirut
«بيريز يهدد بضرب بيروت»

Hitler: I made a mistake by not apprising the importance of American support

قتلر : غلطتي إني ما عرّفتش أهمية الدعم الأمريكي

Al-Goumhouriya, April 24, 1996

Al Goumhouriya, 24 April 1996
Today Sharon is the figure depicted as the personification of evil incarnate, but in their time it was Barak and Peres that were stigmatised in the most scandalous manner

BRAVOOO

Baha Boukhari, montage, *amin.org/cartoon/baha*

Jalal Al-Rifai, *Ad Dustour* (Jordan), 16 May 2006

Gomaa, *Al-Ahram Weekly Online* (Egypt),
12–18 October 2000
Hitler, Sharon and Barak as accomplices in the murder of young Mohammed Al Durah

Al Ahali (Egypt), 20 December 2001
Le soldat-: 'When I've finished with him, I'll take care of you!'

Welcome to Gaza Strip or the Israeli Extermination Camp of Palestinian Refugees
Emad Hajjaj, *Al Quds Al-Arabi* (London), 15 June 2004

Sharon in Jabalya
Stavro Jabra, *Ad Dabbour* (Lebanon), 11 March 2003

Tammam Darwish, *Al Ayyam* (Yemen), 5 August 2006

Fathy, *Al Ahram weekly online* (Egypt), 20–26 July 2006

Al Wifar (Iran), 8 January

Abdurahman Alattas (Indonesia) for the International Cartoon Festival on Occupation, Iran 2006. Note that the artist depicts the Jew as a demoniac beast, even when persecuted by the Nazis.

10. Israel, a treacherous country that does not want peace and is responsible for all the misfortunes in the Arab world (=scapegoat)

Jews are liars. The 'peace process' must be denounced as it is nothing more than an Israeli stratagem intended to destroy the Arabs. We believe the Israelis do not like taking risks, because the Jewish brain is fearful. Adventure is not their line, they prefer conspiracy.
(From the official daily of the Palestine Authority, *Al-Hayat Al-Jadida*, 27 July 1997)

Yet again the Jewish state is portrayed as a criminal and child-slaughtering state, that is not to be trusted at any cost. These cartoons deal with the subject of the treacherous, lying and swindling Jew, beloved of a particular Muslim tradition. Nowadays it is customary to hold the Jews (and the crusaders) responsible for the backward state of the Arab world. If the Muslim world is in crisis it is because of the Israelis. This attitude – of complete victimisation – pays off because it completely absolves the Arab elites and removes them out of the frame.

Goma, *Al Ahram weekly online* (Egypt), 8–14 November 2001

Rasmy, *Arabia.com*, 7 October 2001
'Ceasefire agreement'

Rasmy, *Arabia.com*, 28 May 2001
'Darwin's theory'

Rasmy, *Arabia.com*, 23 September 2001
Palestinian: *'I'm dropping my gun so you believe me.'*
Israeli: *'Now I believe you.'*

Al Thawra (Syria), 1 October 1998
The Oslo Accords

Israel responsible for the Iraq War

Easen Alkalel, *Al Watan* (Oman), 18 May 2004

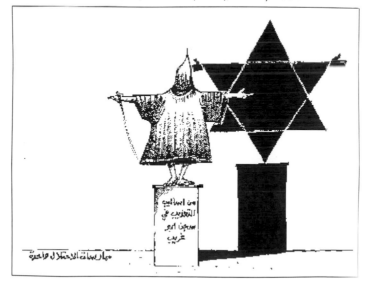

Wherever there is an occupation, there's torture and abuse,
whether it is in Palestine or in Iraq
Hamed Ata, *Akhbar Al-Khaleej* (Bahrain), 7 May 2004

Israel whipping Arab states, one after another, to follow the US in the Israeli 'War on Terror'
Emad Hajjaj, *Al-Quds Al-Arabi* (London), 9 September 2004

Mahragy, *Akhbar Al-Khaleej* (Bahrain), 19 March 2004
The cartoon's headline: 'The Kurds in Iraq'. At the bottom: 'How
easy it is to light the fire, and how difficult it is to extinguish it'.
The US and Israel (the Star of David), represented by a snake, are
going through Syria and igniting a civil war in Kamishly (the Kurdish region in northern Syria).

Yassin Al-Khalil, *Teshreen*, 17 February 2005
Assassination of Al-Hariri

Antisemitism: a typical inversion phenomenon

Easen Alkalel, *Al Watan* (Oman), February 2004
The cartoon's headline: 'The feast of Immolation'. On the right, in Arabic *'The Islamic world's attitude?'*

Samer, *Yemen Times* (Yemen), 29 June 2004

Samer, *Yemen Times* (Yemen), 23 June 2003

Goma, *Al Ahram weekly online* (Egypt),
18–24 November 2004

How Arabs and Israelis are different is demonstrated in how they use
satellites orbiting Earth: the Israelis are using them for spying but Arab
rulers are using them for entertainment purposes.
Mustafa Rahmeh, *Al Ittihad* (UAE), 6 October 2004

Akram Reslan, *Al Yom* (Saudi Arabia), 25 April 2006

Elie Saliba, *Al-Watan* (Qatar), 10 June 2006

Elie Saliba, *Al-Watan* (Qatar), 18 March 2006
Even the 2006 football World Cup is used against 'Israel'

11. The Jew/Israeli is a satanic creature that must be eliminated in order to save humanity

If every Arab killed one Jew, there would be no Jews left.
(Moustafa Tlass, Syrian minister of defence, on LBC radio, 5 May 2001)

On 10 September 2001, the day before the murderous attacks on New York and Washington, the artist Rasmy (opposite) issued an apologia in defence of suicide attacks. Given the content of the cartoons we have seen up to now, this approach appears entirely logical. What other way to treat those who kill children? Of all the hundreds we looked at, we didn't find a single one featuring an Israeli civilian victim. This suggests that the Zionist enemy, always portrayed as a soldier or a 'Hassid', has neither father, mother or child.

Omayya Joha (Palestine),
http://www.omayya.com/new/photogallery/photo041/9.jpg

If the cartoons that follow are not antisemitic in the accepted sense of the word, they are none the less incitements to murder. Death appears logical as the sole punishment to be meted out to the Zionist enemy.

As Pierre-André Taguieff has said, the new Judeophobia in its Islamist-jihadist form is explicitly exterminatory. It defines its struggle as an enterprise dedicated to the total elimination of those that belong to the ultimate enemy.

Rasmy (Jordan), *Arabia.com*, 19 August 2001

Rasmy (Jordan), *Arabia.com*, 20 March 2001

Rasmy (Jordan), Arabia.com, 7 March 2001
'If I tell you that you will see me a second time, it's a lie'

Rasmy, *Arabia.com*, 7 March 2001
To a Russian immigrant: *'Come into my arms!'*

Hamed, *Al Ittihad* (UAE), 12 January 2004
*'The most merciful sentence for my client [Ariel Sharon]
is the death penalty'*

Elie Saliba (Lebanon), *Al Watan* (Qatar), 18 March 2006

Soleman Al Malek, *Al Watan* (Qatar), 7 August 2006

Nedal Deep (Syria), *Arabcartoon*, third week of July 2006

Mohamed Effat Ismail (Egypt), *Arabcartoon*,
third week of July 2006

Yaser Ahmad, *Syria News*, 7 July 2006

Baha Boukhari, *Al Ayyam* (Palestine), 2 August 2006

Mohammad Massod (Yemen), *Arabcartoon*, fifth week of July 2006

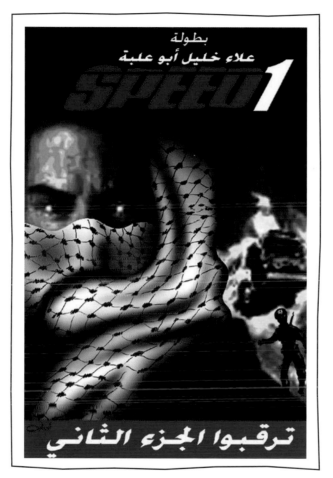

The systematic exploitation of the most classic antisemitic themes essentially reflects the confusion into which successive defeats have plunged the Arab world. In the space of a few years the Arab cartoonists have fallen into a kind of characteristic regression, of which the prototype appears to us to be the French confusion following their defeat in 1870. At once humiliated and obsessed by the desire for revenge, the French cartoons of the period portrayed Germany as a bestial ogre, satanic and vampire-like. These cartoons were as much a call for vengeance as for outright murder, the Teuton no longer really belonging to the human race. Contemporary Arab cartoons are prompted in our opinion by the same phe-

Osama Hajjaj, reworked version of poster advertising the film *Speed*, 17 February 2002.
In the background, an attack on a (civilian) Israeli bus.

nomenon, and this undoubtedly in an intensified form, given the image of the Jews in the Arab-Muslim imagination. The images in the Arab press simply reveal the subconscious urges unleashed by the trauma of the second *intifada*. The stereotypes and symbolic attributes they portray are evidence of this – menacing omnipresence of Death, references to cannibal and vampire fantasies, accusations of child murder, allusions to the scheming of the enemy Satan, that incite to no less than complete and utter destruction. All these intertwined themes indisputably demonstrate the difficulty of the Arab world in accepting the idea of a Jewish state in the middle of the Arab world.

Chapter 4

Return of the myth of the Jews as ogres and vampires

The preceding cartoons may have been surprising. The image of Jews that they convey are in fact based upon stereotypes that decent people had believed obsolete at the beginning of the third millennium. Jews in the Arab Muslim press appear to have been lifted straight from prints and almanacs of times gone by, even from collaborationist newspapers or from the Hitler period. From being drinkers of Aryan blood, as they were dubbed by Rosenberg, the Nazi proponent of racial theory, they have now become vampires of the Palestinian people, and insatiable assassins of Arab children.

Exploitation of the martyrdom of Palestinian children

From the repeated and insistent nature of these representations, these accusations, it is evident that they are quite clearly not, as some maintain, the result of mistaken deduction or the product of a simple blunder. Unfortunately they are part of a deliberate and conscious strategy. For proof of this all it needs is to surf the web and visit the Palestinian propaganda sites. *Intifada.com*, available in at least thirteen languages, is one of these sites. One of these pages supporting the second intifada and entitled 'Innocence assassinated' reads as follows:

Palestinians do not enjoy a normal childhood … How do you teach children about the goodness of human nature, when they see before their eyes the worst examples of human beings? … Palestinian psychologists are deeply discouraged. In an interview on French television one of them expressed his

inability to convince these children of the inherent goodness within human nature.[66]

If we are to believe *Intifada.com*, the Israelis are '*the worst example of human beings*' and the theme is repeated and developed on dozens of other sites across the internet.

The war crimes, the assassinations, the torture and extortion of children are all specialities of the IDF (Israel Defence Forces). Deliberately targeting children is one of the most grotesque but also the most typical feature of the Israeli policy of ethnic cleansing in the Occupied Territories. Quite apart from the horrific nature of these atrocities constituting direct violations of international law, the fact is that they take it out on children in every conceivable way.[67]

In support of this assertion they do not moreover shrink from resorting to the most vile, the most insane accusations, such as for example the theft of bodily organs, a crime that Jews have been accused of since the Middle Ages. On 24 December, 2001, a date not without significance, the official daily newspaper of the Palestinian Authority accused the Israelis of using Palestinian body parts for evil purposes:

When the occupying authorities take possession of the bodies of martyrs, it is in order to remove all traces of their crimes. Witnesses and evidence prove that the occupying forces deliberately torture the bodies of these martyrs and even finish them off by shooting… There is clear evidence indicating that body parts of martyrs are taken while they are in custody, particularly for Israeli patients in need of transplants. After removing body parts from martyrs, [Israeli authorities] bury the corpses in

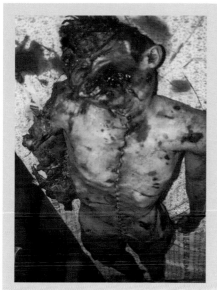

If this is the truth, then God bless Israel

By cee@post.com 10:25am Thursday Jan 17'02

Modified at 4 :56 Friday Jan 18'02

http://www.webspawner.com/users/horroagain/Index.html

cee@post.com

Kidnapped, Tortured, Killed, Mutilated, and Used as spare parts (english) by A Picture 10:55am Wed Jan 16 '02 (Modified on 8:22pm Wed Jan 16 '02) A new Israeli Massacre was committed against three innocent kids in Palestine.
The three kids were kidnapped two days ago. They were tortured and brutally killed. Their inner vital organs such as Heart, Kidney and Liver were taken away to be used in Jewish bodies. The Israeli monsters dropped their dead bodies near Sheikh Radwan Palestinian Refugee Camp in the Gaza Strip.

NOT FOR CHILDREN! SHOOKING HORROR!

suspicious circumstances in defiance of humanitarian values and moral and religious law. Legal authorities indicate that the refusal of the occupiers to restore the bodies of martyrs to their families is intended to hide the truth of the inhumane practices carried out on the bodies of martyrs…[68]

No sooner is it issued than the antisemitic message immedi ately finds its target and expands: on 17 January 2002 alleged 'photographs' were broadcast on a global scale, this time via the net, of children's corpses dismembered by the Israelis. Admittedly crude accusations, faked and corrupted documents they may have been, but the images were unbearable, hence eminently saleable. False as it was the information was relayed by a number of progressive media, among others the Belgian, Catalan and Californian sections of the chief anti-globalisation press agency, *Indymedia*.[69] Reprinted above is the web page that conveyed the accusation in Belgium. By nature of the imputations it expresses and with its 'visual'- in today's parlance - it plunges us straight back into … the twelfth century. Note the passionate, even theological tone of the heading, *'If this is the truth, then God bless Israel'*.[70]

The very fact that one of the media describing itself as on the left should pass on a rumour of such dimensions, which it did without finding it necessary to verify the information and confirm its sources, as if this information stood by itself, is a clear indication of the return of leftist antisemitism. In defence of the Palestinians, it must however be said that this calumny was denounced by the Palestinian League of the Rights of Man:

Indymedia is an electronic mass media, fiercely anti-globalisation. It is a powerful international organisation with hundreds of thousands of supporters worldwide – somewhat on the model of Greenpeace, but judging by some of the pages appearing on its web sites, less dignified in style, with a strong tendency towards denigration and use of simplistic, even Manichaean arguments and sometimes resorting to really violent language. These people exchange ideas, share information and broadcast it on a truly massive scale (there are dozens of national sites throughout the world under the name of Indymedia). They instigate communal large-scale actions, with a huge organisational capacity. By means of this covert form of action they have mobilised thousands of militants to boycott the meetings of the G7 and G8 and others of a similar order, for example at Seattle and Genoa in 2001. The fact that on their own account they have produced such a crude slander, supported by clichés intended to demonise the Israelis, for allegedly having committed these crimes – and all this without the slightest attempt at verifying the accuracy of these facts – is no credit to their fight against globalisation of the economy. Freedom of expression and thought is not an excuse for everything. We expect those responsible and members of Indymedia to repudiate this libellous campaign and take action so that these shameful pages are removed immediately from the sites concerned.[71]

The blood libel: the key theme of anti-Zionist propaganda

The rumour put about by *Indymedia* in a climate where criticism of a state, rightly or wrongly judged to be an oppressor, is founded not on logical or verifiable arguments but on fables feeding on a medieval, mythical arsenal. Yet again the Israelis, since it is they that are the targets, are being accused of taking it out on the most innocent of innocents – children. Here we have a return to the subjects and clichés that became taboo – in certain circles at least – with the traumas following the Second World War: the unleashing of fantasies that had previously been more or less contained. What other interpretation is there of the special issue of an authentic Belgian pacifist magazine, *Les Sentiers de la paix (The Paths of Peace)* dated July 2001 (nos.28–29) with a cover picture of a Palestinian child behind barbed wire? The icon is a striking one. The captions selected by *Les Sentiers de la paix* to accompany the images are no less eloquent –here is an example.

The same idea underlies the *Student Association of the State University of San Francisco*'s campaign of April 2002. The very

A cover symptomatic of a particular view of the conflict.

Right: The caption to this photo of three young boys playing reads: 'Here in Gaza we need to bear lots of children… because they're likely to be killed every day! (Palestinian woman)'

least that can be said is that the poster, with both the GUPS (General Union of Palestinian Students) and the MSA (Association of Muslim Students) as co-signatories, is that it appeals to the judeophobic imagination.[71] With its representation of a tin of a 'Palestinian children's meat' the poster accuses the Israelis and denounces Judaism at one and the same time. After all, aren't Arab children slaughtered *'for Jewish ritual purposes'*?

The time has come for fierce all-round condemnation, including the boycott of alleged Israeli products.

San Francisco, April 2002: return to the myth of the cannibalistic Jew.
The meat is kosher, as the children have been slaughtered *'according to Jewish rites'*.

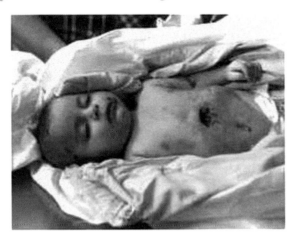

next time you see

Johnson & Johnson

Remember this Baby

This baby was killed by an Israeli sharpshooter, notice how he has carefully centred his aim before releasing the the trigger.

Companies like Johnson & Johnson keep the Israeli war machine going. On Israels 50th Anniversary, Johnson & Johnson was awarded Israels highest tribute - the Jubilee Award, in recognition for its continued service in strengthening the Israeli economy.

BOYCOTT ISRAEL

www.inminds.co.uk, 2002
This specific iconography refers to the martyrdom of Christ. The Palestinian baby's wounds here recall the stigmata of the crucified Jesus.

Plus jamais ça!

BOYCOTT ISRAEL
www.islamiya.net

Never again! (www.islamiya.net and www.boycotter-israel.fr.st)

Qu'ai-je fait pour mériter toute cette galère ?

BOYCOTT ISRAEL
www.islamiya.net

What have I done to deserve all this? (www.islamiya.net and www.boycotter-israel.fr.st)

The boycott of Jewish (?) products serves to rerun the drama of the child-murdering Jew
(*www.inminds.co.uk*, 2002)

Holywar.com, one of the most extreme Christian far right websites, exploits Palestinian children to attack the Jewish state by means of a campaign boycotting Israeli products

On 24 June 2003, during its campaign for a boycott of Israeli fruits and vegetables, Oxfam Belgium produced a poster representing a bleeding 'Israeli' orange, which could be construed as suggesting the medieval blood libel. The poster was removed following protests by the Simon Wiesenthal Center. Oxfam International issued an apology.

A campaign against a company that had in fact itself boycotted
the Israeli market for many years to avoid alienating the Arab
world
(*www.inminds.co.uk*, 2002)

*Has anyone out there stopped to think what effect the daily horrors in Palestine are having on the children there? For many of them it seems the
norm as their young parents went through the same horrors... victims of the same beasts.*
Justice is long overdue for this glorious nation. The concepts of peace and justice are alien to an entire generation... this has to change NOW!
Palestine must be free and must be allowed to prosper like any other nation. FREEDOM NOW!
Ben Heine (Belgium) for the Cartoon and 'Desertpeace' for the text, http//desertpeace.blogspot.com.

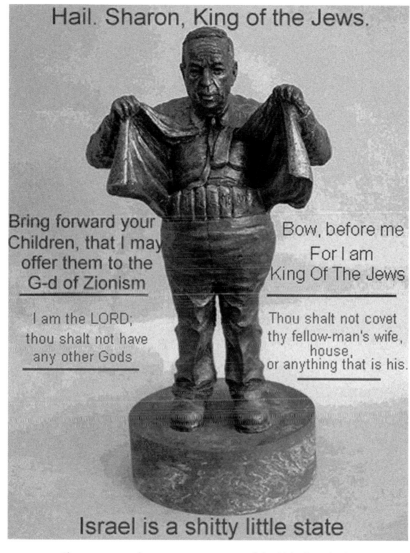

Sharon appears here as a reincarnation of the Moloch myth, dear to nineteenth-century Christian antisemites. He is shown wearing a belt of explosives. Also included on the poster are two of the Ten Commandments (2002).

Herzl, founder of the Zionist state (2002). Again the use of the blood
libel and ritual murder 'antisemyths' against Israel.

The Jews and Israel in press cartoons: a return to the most hackneyed of clichés?

Our central thesis, taken from Uriel Reshef, is well known: in periods of political and ideological instability, stereotypes, dreams and myths surface from deep down in the human psyche and emerge in the field of consciousness. How else does one decipher certain cartoons published in the Western media since the launch of the second *intifada*, such as, for example, the drawings of the Belgian *Nicolas Vadot* (in *Le Vif-L'Express*) and by Serguei (in *Le Monde*) reproduced below? We wouldn't dream of ascribing the merest hint of antisemitism to these three excellent cartoonists. Our intention is to highlight the simplifications, at times isolated, but in our eyes, abusive and dangerous.

Are the cartoons of Serguei, Willem and Kroll innocent and neutral? Absolutely not.

Even if our three cartoonists are not consciously prejudiced, their graphic vocabulary, whether intentionally or not derives from a Judeophobic tradition that is as ancient as it is archetypal (cf. the Golgotha).

What else can be said of the two cartoons by Willem that appeared in *Libération*

at the height of the second *intifada*, other than that they take their inspiration from an indisputably anti-Jewish source? This is what prompted Clément Weill-Raynal, French Radio 3 journalist and president of the Association

Israeli soldier (Sharon?) facing Palestinian children
Serguei, *Le Monde*, 2 August 2002

of Jewish Journalists of the French Press, to say to Jacques Amalric, editorial director of *Libération*:

> Just one question: What is the connection between kosher meat and Ariel Sharon? What does a dietary law observed by Jews for thousands of years have to do with the politics of the new prime minister of Israel?

Lâchez votre arme, ou ce sera l'escalade!

Nicolas Vadot, *Le Vif-l'Express*, 20 April 2001. *Drop your arms, or things will escalate!* The mass graves of Bergen Belsen and Dachau (1944) are what subconsciously feed the imagery of the Arab–Israeli conflict.

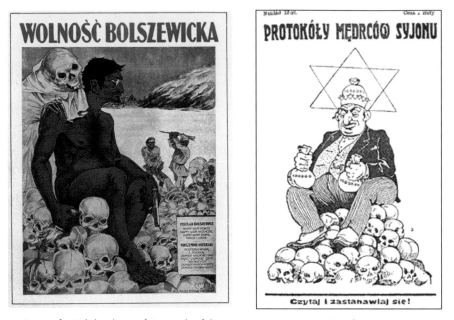

Cover of a Polish edition of *Protocols of the Elders of Zion* published during the Nazi occupation, Poznan, 1943

Trotsky, Polish propaganda poster, 1920

"Our policy of selective executions is starting to bear fruit!"

Canada, December 2001

Clearly, during the 1920s it was not Sharon sitting enthroned on his ossuary, but another 'war criminal', another Jew

118

Dave Brown's cartoon, which was published in the London *Independent*, depicts Israeli Prime Minister Ariel Sharon eating a baby. Is this cartoon antisemitic or solely anti-Israeli? For Dave Brown the answer is simple: his cartoon is just inspired by a famous painting by Goya, *'Saturn eating his own children'*. Its purpose: denounce Ariel Sharon's brutal policy. In fact the answer is complex. In a sense, it depends on what Sharon is actually eating: an Israeli baby or a Palestinian one? If the child is Palestinian (which seems to be the case, Sharon being in Gaza), it couldn't be considered as a reinterpretation of Goya but as a reminiscence of the medieval blood libel charges against the Jews. Saturn eats his own children! If the child is Israeli, the question stays open, even if we can question why Jews (here its prime minister) are always connected to infanticide. Of course, the question is not to determine if Brown is an antisemite – we do not believe he is – but to demonstrate that his drawing carries an antisemitic charge.

Francisco Goya (1748–1828)
Saturn eating his own children

Willem, *Libération* (France), 7 February 2001
Arafat: *'It's not even kosher.'*
Sharon: *'No one's asking you.'*

Willem, *Libération* (France), 26 December 2001
Title: *No Christmas for Arafat.*
Sharon: *But for Easter, he is welcome.*

Willem cannot be suspected of Jew-hatred,[75] we are fully aware of this, but his two cartoons are unacceptable in the sense that the political message they proclaim does not rest on an ensemble of witnessed facts, but on rumours feeding on the power of strong images continuing down the centuries. Let us turn back again to the comments of Elie Barnavi:

I have before me the cartoon by Willem of 26 December... At the moment of writing these lines, a terrible doubt is gnawing at me – what if the afore-mentioned readers of *Libé* prove – in these secular times – unable to appreciate this evangelical allusion? ... Here we are again. Easter, the Passion of Christ. And just as the ancestors of Sharon, in long-ago Judea (but wasn't that Palestine, even then?) crucified Jesus, the prime minister of Israel will crucify Arafat, the new Christ. I can already hear the chorus of hypocrites – what, is no one allowed to criticisze Israel? How is it that every time you disagree with the government of Israel, they trot out the hackneyed accusation of antisemitism? Well, actually yes, dear Philistines, you are perfectly entitled to criticize Sharon time and again, and all his ministers as well, and me into the bargain. You may think what you like about the decision to prevent Arafat, the good apostle, from going to Bethlehem, to say so, to write it, to shout it at the top of your voices. What's more no one is prevented from doing so in Israel, either, even on the government benches. But the Cross, gentlemen, the Cross…[76]

Willem is not the only one to risk producing drawings that challenged the boundaries of what was regarded as acceptable.

We can hear the objections from here. Are the Jews to be untouchable then? Isn't a humourist entitled to insert a butcher's cleaver into the hands of a paper Sharon, stain him with the blood of his victims, or make him nail Arafat up on to a Christian cross, without automatically being taken for an enemy of mankind, for an appalling antisemite? Broadly speaking, why is it permissible to depict Milosevic dismembering children, and not Sharon? Are the Jews made of different stuff than the Serbs? Are they entitled to special laws? To a right to being drawn in a way appropriate to them? It

is true that at the time of the war in Bosnia, Plantu resorted to the subject of crucifixion and infanticide in order to denounce the atrocities committed by the Serbian troops (there were at least 200,000 Bosnian victims). It is no less true to say that Plantu has never used such themes against Sharon – for whom he has no great liking, however, and denounces in as many other ways as possible. Apart from the sufferings of the Palestinian people, he, Plantu, knows full well that there are comparisons, allusions and images that he simply cannot use. As a result of which he refrains – whether as a joke, or in favour of a 'just cause' – from associating Jews with money, Jews with blood, Jews with the death of Christ. Many of his colleagues unfortunately lack this understanding and decency…

Kroll *In Le Soir*, 25th December 2002 (reprint)
April 2002, Bethlehem, siege of the Church of the Nativity. Soldier on the right: *'Anything to eat in there, d'you think?* Soldier with binoculars: *'Not a lot - a cow and a donkey'.*
Kroll is a talented cartoonist, and yet his image still tends towards making Jesus take the role of a Palestinian, and hence the Israelis as Romans.

Le Kroll

18th December 2006
An 'Israeli' observing inter Palestinian fights in the Gaza Strip

'But how can they treat me this way after all I've done for them...?
Giorgio Forattini, *Panorama* (Italy), 13 December 2002.
It's obvious that the Jews don't hesitate to crucify their allies.

The fact is that by refusing to submit to the martyrdom threatened by the coalition of Arab armies in 1948, and then by winning the 1967 war, the Jews in Israel shed that virginity which more than one of their alleged friends set so much store by; in throwing off this dedication to misfortune that suited them so well they, as it were, betrayed their nature, their mission. This 'abandonment' which required the post-Shoah Jews, those in Israel and others elsewhere, to cast off the bespoke garments that the Christian West had at one time fitted them out with, making them a separate people, indifferent to the fate of others, egotistical, cruel and capable of deicide; having suffered martyrdom themselves, they in turn became the crucifiers. Moreover, cannot their present conduct be attributed to the wretched treatment meted out to them over the centuries? There are those that do not shrink from asking this question.

Memory of Sacrifice, Serguei, *Le Monde*, 26 July 2006.
Serguei is a very talented cartoonist but why always associate the Jewish people with deicide and, even more, here, (the Jew) Jesus with the... Hezbollah?

Giorgio Forattini, *La Stampa* (Italy), 3 April 2002
Jesus in Bethlehem: 'Are they going to kill me again?'

Frano Cebalo (Croatia)[13]

Zak, *De Morgen* (Flemish socialist daily), 6 April 2002
Heading: 'Palestinians barricaded in the Church of the Nativity'
Palestinian: 'Well, here we are'
Christ on the Cross replies: 'Don't talk to ME about the Jews!'

Andreas Molau in both the organ of the NPD
(*Deutsche Stimme*, September 2006) and *Iran cartoon*.
Again an image that tends to place the Jews in the Romans' role. Here
Olmert as Pontius Pilate to the great joy of the German neo-fascist party.

Rainer Hachfeld in the post-Communist *Neues Deutschland* draws a
heavily 'Jewified' Sharon, kippah and all, receiving a cornucopia
of gifts from Schröder and Fischer.

Gustavo Munoz Matiz, in *Solidaire*, organ of the (Maoist) Parti du Travail de Belgique (PTB). Even the Marxist-Leninists do not hesistate to play with christic symbol
and... prejudice (i.e. deicide).

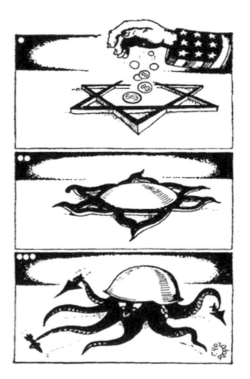

Gennady Chegodayev (2002, Russia), *Irancartoon.ir*

124

The Shoah 'versus' Israel (I)

Another previously untouchable subject has opened up: it looks as if the Shoah no longer has the power to keep antisemitic feelings at bay. There is in fact evidence that across the board, from the far right to the far left, there are those that take advantage of the 'opportunity' offered by the Israeli–Palestinian conflict to unleash antisemitic utterances long suppressed precisely on account of the genocide.

What has not however been stated, on the other hand, is that this same genocide has recently begun to appear as a trigger for antisemitism.

Furthermore, it seems to us that the hostility towards Israel could be due at least in part to an attitude of mind that requires Israelis and Jews to be blameless models of morality. This elitist assumption, paradoxically tinged with a slight hint of anti-Arab racism, maintains that the Jews as heirs of a three-thousand year old civilisation are subject to far stricter moral obligations than their enemies. But what explanation is there for demanding more from the Jews than from ordinary mortals, other than an inverted form of racism? And why push criticism so far, to the point of comparing the Israelis with their Nazi executioners as in this cartoon by Gado published on 1 May 2002 in *Le Monde*?[79]

One is entitled – some might say there is a duty – to criticise Israeli military operations, but why these systematic allusions to the Shoah?

The temptation to replace the emotive accusation of the holocaust with a radical criticism of Israel is becoming ever more explicit. The notion, cherished by Abbé Pierre, the most popular Frenchman according to opinion polls, according to whom '*from being victims the Jews have become executioners*' has rapidly emerged in the minds of good souls who, though not necessarily inveterate and outspoken enemies of the Jews, nevertheless feel irritation, distrust and a kind of general antipathy towards them. Not knowing what to make of this awkward feeling that confounds them in the very special context of the post-Shoah era, they seize upon the first argument likely to provide a logical foundation for this 'intellectual anomaly', an objective justification and a certain dignity. This attitude flourishes all the more readily on soil – that of classic anti-Jewishness – that is fresh and fertile.

Thus, it seems to us, that anti-Zionism would appear to have become a means of drowning a feeling of vague guilt on the part of the West towards the Jews not long since abandoned to barbarity, a neat way of making up for the cowardliness and abandonment of the past by taking up an unambiguous and virtuous position on behalf of the victims of major contemporary injustices. An attitude far more resolute in the case under discussion than towards all the victims in a world so rich in reprobates, inequalities, fratricidal wars, undeclared colonial wars, attempted ethnocide or acknowledged genocide, from the Sudan to Tibet, by way of Chechnya or Rwanda; yet it is the Palestinians that attract the maximum sympathy. As if by chance, one might be tempted to say, these people being precisely those that present themselves to the conscience of the world as the victims of those very ones, the Jews, who on the other hand evoke a feeling of unease in view of the way they were abandoned. So why then the Palestinians, and not the Sudanese or the Chechens? Does anyone ever ask?

Weren't France, and Belgium too, complicit in the genocide of the Tutsis in 1994? Let's not forget the disastrous toll: one million dead in 100 days, something like 10,000 victims per day. And at the time what were the Christian organisations doing, quick as they are to denounce the situation in the territories occupied by Israel, but supporting the genocidal Hutus on a massive and incomprehensible scale?

Godfrey Mwampembwa ('Gado'), *Nation* (Kenya), 25 April 2002. This cartoon was reprinted by *Le Monde* (France) in May.
In each of the sketches that make up this drawing, a figure holds his head in his hands and weeps against a background of ruin and rubble.
Left: '*Warsaw 1943*'. Right: '*Jenin today*'.
Were the official excuses issued enough to banish the feeling of unease in the face of this 'absurd comparison' (in the words of *Le Monde*).
500,000 perished in Warsaw; 78 in Jenin, of whom 23 were Israeli soldiers.

Back in 1971 in his introduction to *L'Imprescriptible*, Vladimir Jankelevitch already denounced the link between antisemitism and the Shoah:

This shameful secret that we are not allowed to utter is the secret of the Second World War, and to some extent the secret of modern man: it is the immense holocaust – even if it is not spoken of – that weighs on our modernity in the form of invisible remorse. How are we to shake it off? This title of a play by Ionesco characterises the anxieties behind the apparent ease of the contemporary conscience. The crime was too serious, the responsibility too great, observes Rabi with cruel lucidity. How can they rid themselves of their latent remorse? 'Anti-Zionism' is a godsend in this respect for it gives us permission, even

PAST AND ...   ...PRESENT

Petar Pismestrovic, *Kleine Zeitung* (Austria), May 2004.
Whatever one's view of Israeli policies, this comparison is inappropriate and offensive. The cartoon is particularly offensive coming from an Austrian newspaper, considering Austria's past.

Miroslaw Hajnos (2002, Poland),
Irancartoon.ir[77]

WRITE THIS ONE IN YOUR DIARY ANNE!

Finn Graff, *Dagbladet* (Norway), 10 July 2006.
Israeli Prime Minister Ehud Olmert is caricatured as the infamous Nazi concentration camp commander depicted in the film *Schindler's List*, who shot random Jewish prisoners for sport.

Cartoon made by 'Nabucho' for the *Arab European League* (Belgium), 2 February 2006,
http://www.arabeuropean.org/newsdetail.php?ID=95

Forever comparing with the Shoah! Clio, muse of history, *putting Hitler's moustache on Ariel Sharon.*
Forges, *El Pais* (Spain), 23 May 2001.

Steve Bell, *Guardian*, 7 February 2001

gives us the right and even imposes the duty to be antisemites in the name of democracy! Ant-Zionism is justified antisemitism available to all. It is the permission to be a democratic antisemite. And what if the Jews were themselves Nazis? That would be marvellous. Then they would no longer need to be pitied; they would have deserved their fate. This is the way our contemporaries shake off their concern. For any alibi will do that can at last leave them free to think of other things.[80]

Alain Finkielkraut goes further: 'For progressive Europeans we are the scum of the earth. They compare the Jewish state to a Nazi state. In their view you cannot defend a Nazi state without being a Nazi yourself, and from the perspective of peace you cannot criticize certain Palestinian politicians. This represents a new episode in the totalitarian aberrations of intellectuals.' In a word: 'The swastika is our next yellow star.[81]'

In Belgium Sharon was systematically presented as one of the biggest war criminals of… all time. Here Royer in *Le Soir*, the main Francophone newspaper.
'Next Affair.'
'Bring in the defendant, Attila King of the Huns.'

The Shoah 'versus' Israel (II): the strange case of Greece[82]

Dimitris Hantzopoulos, *Ta Nea* (one of the main Greek papers),
1 April 2002
*'I'm not bothered about doing to you what the Nazis did to us.
What upsets me is that your people are doing to us what I'm
about to do to you.'*

Toliadis, *Ethnos* (centre left Greek daily, close to the
government)[7] April 2002
*'Don't feel guilty, brother. We didn't go to Auschwitz and
Dachau to suffer, we went there to learn.'*

'To slaughter or to kill ? That is the question'
Epohi, 7 April 2002

Spiros Ornerakis, *Ta Nea*, 2 April 2002

Cover of bi-monthly magazine of Thessaloniki, *VIP*, April 2002. Note that the powder coming out of the bag has the shape of skull heads.

Stathis, *Eleftherotypia*, 30 March 2002
'At last, completed things! As we killed the Jews then… now the Israelis are killing the memory of the killed… [Warsaw Ghetto 1944 - Ramallah 2002]'. Of course, the ghetto insurrection was in 1943, not 1944 but what could we expect from an 'expert' like Stathis?

'*Holocaust II*' cover page of *Eleftherotypia* by Kyr, 1 April 2002
Blatant reversal of the well-known image of the child in the ghetto

Yiannis Kalaitzis, *Eleftherotypia*, 11 April 2002
*'My policy has reached a dead end. The way I am going, I won't have any
Palestinians left to slaughter.'*

Stathis Stavropoulos, *Eleftherotypia*, 24 September 2002
'Arafat is no longer an interlocutor of the Reich.'
'Why is he Jewish?'

Return of the myth of the Jews as ogres and vampires

Stathis Stavropoulos, *Eleftherotypia*, 11 April 2002
'Whoever was killed by bad Ariel Sharon and bad George Bush should go to the right... whoever was killed by good Shimon Peres and good Colin Powell should go to the left...'
What the Israeli does is worse than what the Nazis did in Auschwitz: the two lines bring to death! Note too that the so-called leftist Stathis does not hesitate to play with the most antisemitic symbol: the deicide (three crosses)!

Stathis Stavropoulos, *Eleftherotypia*, 13 September 2004
'We should deport them!   No, wall them!
Murder them!   No, kill them!
Eliminate them!   No, scatter them!
Even I start to find disagreements a component of democracy!'

Stathis pushes the perversion to put on the American soldier's helmet the Jewish star and on the Israeli one... the swastika.

'Fear in the Fourth Reich'
Stathis, *Eleftherotypia*, August 2006

Eleftherotypia, 19 July 2006
Butcher's shop 'The Good Heart', E. Olmert
Butcher: 'We Kostas [Karamanlis, Greek PM] against terrorism we implement the Greek method. If he is a 50% suspect we cut 50%, if he a 20% suspect we cut 20%, plus VAT, social security and other expenses.' The kid pulling a book titled 'Marx & Spencer' is meant to be Greek PM Kostas Karamanlis. The back of his shirt reads 'Non-permanent member [of the Security Council].'

Eleftherotypia, 12 July 2006
Butcher: 'What I do with the Palestinians is my business. What do you want?'
Client (USA, described as USASS): '2 kilos of lamb chops, some liver, a head and half a kilo of minced meat.' Note: On the upper right hand side there is a vertical message which states 'Butcher shop widely accepted.' The word 'widely' in Greek (Evreos) is purposely misspelled as Evraios (Jew) which sounds exactly the same, using a play on words.

The Shoah 'versus' Israel (III): the case of Carlos Latuff

Of course, the new anti-Zionists do not have the same exterminating hatred towards Jews on an individual level in the same way as the Nazis, far from it! Nevertheless, like it or not, they are playing a dangerous game in reviving images that are anything but innocent. The process is all the more absurd since the criticisms they hurl at Israel are very carefully couched with regard to other states, that are often more guilty as far as human rights are concerned. Along with others, Pascal Perrineau, present director of CEVIPOP (Centre for French Political Studies) and leading French specialist in the phenomenon of racism, he has noted that these same intellectuals are never heard to '*condemn the Islamist version of anti-Zionism that is currently promulgated in thousands of mosques from the Atlantic to the Persian Gulf in the sermons of imams whose call to murder does not distinguish between Jews and Zionists. Anti-Zionism in its different varieties, be they Islamist or Western, is a deadly ideology representing the modern version of the ostracism always suffered by the Jews. In fact, most states have committed – some of them continue to do so – injustices, crimes and atrocities on a far greater scale than those Israel is accused of. But apart from anti-Zionism, nowhere in the world is there any other movement contesting the legitimacy of a state in this way.*'[83]

Pierre André Taguieff has dubbed this phenomenon of exclusively denouncing the State of Israel and its Jewish 'accomplices' as the new 'judeophobia'.[84] Not without reason the French philosopher emphasises how this new attitude relates to a long history of misunderstandings, as well as representing

'*Ariel Sharon secret love*', 28 November 2003

a new phenomenon. This rejection specifically of the Jews is distinct both from the modern form of antisemitism as well as from the traditional and two thousand-year-old Christian anti-Judaism – even though it does share some of the features of the latter. In this context there is the resurgence of the barely disguised accusation of crimes against children (energised by the exploitation of the death of 'little Muhammad' and the repression of the second *intifada*), the notion of a deicidal nation, as well as the cliché of a new perfidy: the suggestion that the one-time victims have in turn become 'executioners'. The Shoah is at the centre of the new way in which the Jews are represented. One press cartoonist, in particular, who concentrates on all those old and new Judeophobic stereotypes, is the anti-globalisation cartoonist Carlos Latuff.

Above all others, the cartoons of Brazilian Carlos Latuff, posted on nearly a hundred sites worldwide, are evidence of the antisemitic drift of authentic progressive militants.[85] The problem is not that Carlos Latuff is pro-Palestinian (he has every right to be so) but that he transforms a conflict that for us is of a national nature into a quasi-eschatological battle with Good opposing Evil, into a conflict of Man confronting the Beast, indeed even worse. The

A typical Latuff caricature: *is this a warrant for genocide?*

Brazilian cartoonist does not hesitate to portray Sharon sometimes as a vampire, sometimes as the Devil incarnate. Not content with making Charles Manson, the Californian psychopath who brutally assassinated the wife of the Jewish film-maker, Roman Polanski, into an officer of Tsahal (sic), he designates him with the number associated with the Anti-Christ, namely 666. Likewise, the globalist cartoonist reprocesses the Shoah solely to the advantage of the Palestinians.

Indymedia.org.uk, 30 June 2002

Carlos Latuff, the contemporary *Drumont* of the internet

Israeli are Born to Kill... babies!
Indymedia.org, 20 June 2002

Is Carlos Latuff judeophobic? This is not the real question. The reality is that he uses medieval and modern antisemitic grammar and vocabulary. Israeli are not "born to kill babies", to suck children blood, connected with evil (666). Latuff is driven by that pure and simple faith of the moralising crusaders and monks of former days. The new 'Christ's people', the true martyred people are the Palestinians – this is the message proclaimed by numbers of his cartoons. Latuff, for whom the notions of 'child people', 'proletarian people' and 'Christ's people' are interchangeable and merge as if by magic, appearing possessed by the Palestinian 'act' and by it alone. Radical and activist Palestine is a source of fascination. It recalls the myth of Che Guevara. The Palestine on the side of Good confronts Evil, the Israeli, born

Sharon victorious as seen by Latuff, *Indymedia Belgium*, 29 January 2003

Indymédia.org, 27 January 2003

Indymedia Belgium, n.d.

to kill, especially babies, as shown on the inscription around the soldier's helmet, with almost no nose, because, as the artist has stated categorically in one of those commentaries he is so adept at, no way would he want to be *'suspected of antisemitism'*. In presenting the Israeli–Palestinian conflict as a straightforward battle between soldiers and civilians, symbolised by small children, Carlos Latuff achieves the impossible of being both anti-racist and antisemitic at one and the same time – in effect he recaptures the classic image of the Jew as child murderer, by redrawing the image that harks back to Herod's *Massacre of the Innocents* down to the alleged ritual murders of medieval times. The drawings and photomontages assembled here typify

Israel began a fifth day of bombardments as part of an operation that followed Hezbollah's capture of two Israeli soldiers. More than 80 Lebanese were killed, including women and children.

I HEARD THAT IN 1942 THE NAZIS MASSACRED CIVILIANS IN LIDICE AS REVENGE FOR THE DEATH OF A NAZI OFFICER!

YES! THE GOOD OL' NAZIS TAUGHT US A LOT...

BEIRUT

'Che Guevara was Palestinian', 23 February 2002.
Good responding to Absolute Evil: the Palestinian cause, a veritable secular religion, is a faith endowed with its own saints, such as the magnificent Palestinian Che, a reincarnation of Christ.

'Palestinian Pietá in Jenin', machination.org, 19 April 2002
The concepts of a people made up of children, proletarians and Christ are superimposed and confused with one another.

'The Virgin seriously wounded by Israeli soldiers', 16 March 2002

'Barak, criminal of the month'
Latuff, October 2000

'Criminal of the month, November 2000' without comment, December 2000. In the eyes of Latuff, the Israeli is first and foremost a soldier who kills for pleasure and not out of duty.

Prior to Sharon, Barak was the target for Latuff's attacks. People tend to ignore the extent to which Barak was also subjected to the most demented attacks. February 2000.

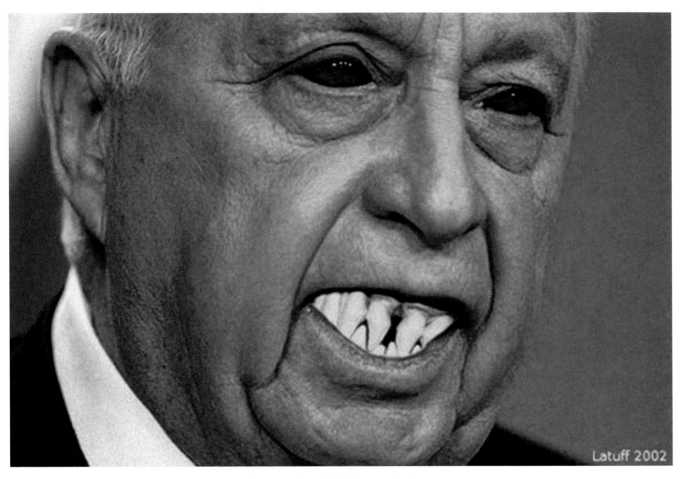

Return to the myth of the vampire Jew.
'His name is terror', photomontage by Latuff, *Indymedia.org*, 3 August 2002. Note that the canines are wrongly placed!

the apparent 'paradoxes' of the new anti-Zionism, which while claiming only to attack Israeli politics, in reality target and revive all the themes of classic anti-Judaism.

If we go back to the underlying problem, it's not that Carlos Latuff is an antisemite obsessed with images from another era (there are others, even on the left) but that he is distributed by a substantial number of progressive sites, most being on the hundreds of local *Indymedia web sites all over the world, includ-*ing *Palestine, Israel, United States, etc.*[86] So whereas he admits that '*Latuff's cartoons have given rise to public debate about the borderline between anti-Zionism and anti-Semitism*,' Gilles Klein, one of the directors of *Indymedia France* considered it equally important to clarify to two journalists on *Le Monde* that he did not anticipate their being censored.[87] Thus the struggle against antisemitism is no longer a sacred issue. Only in *Indymedia Germany* was Carlos Latuff censored, to the great fury of Latuff.

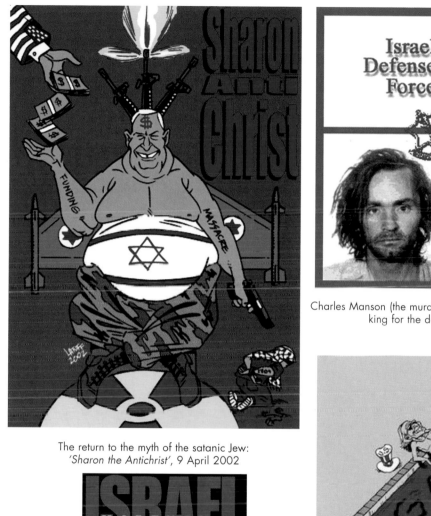

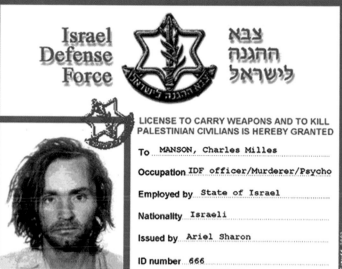

Charles Manson (the murderer of Sharon Tate Polanski) as an IDF officer working for the devil (666), in *44an.com*, Sweden, n.d.

The return to the myth of the satanic Jew:
'Sharon the Antichrist', 9 April 2002

Pure delirium

The Israelis are portrayed as child murderers, the Zionists as shit, and Bush as a whore in the service of Sharon, the Jewish pimp. Latuff is clearly deranged. Yet he nevertheless remains an icon for some anti-globalisation leftist groups. 2002.

The image of suicide bombers is reversed in the Palestinians' favour. Here Sharon himself is shown responsible for the explosion at the Pizzeria in the middle of August 2001, where 16 Israelis including 9 children met their death. 7 February 2002.

2002

'9 terrorists killed by an Israeli F16', Gushshalom, 26 July 2000

'Gaza', 27 June 2006

'From Israel with love', 18 July 2006

'Stop the Zionazi hero', 20 May 2004

'Intifada', 10 January 2005

'New Israeli Flag', n.d.

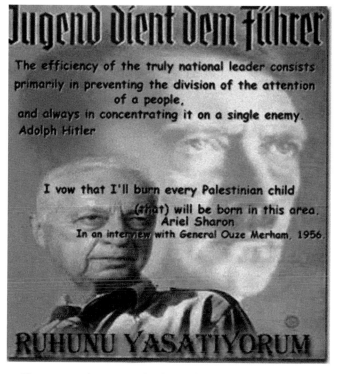

'The young in the service of Hitler'. In this montage assembled by using a Nazi propaganda poster, Latuff starts by quoting Hitler, and goes on to attribute the words to a (fake) Sharon. 'I vow to burn every Palestinian child born in this region'. n.d.

Sharon, the equivalent of Hermann Goering, 2001

'Palestine', 9 March 2006

'*About Mohammed cartoon*', 17 February 2006, presented at the Iranian (anti-)Holocaust competition

'Welcome to Palestine', 44an.com, Sweden, 16 April 2002

Again an explicit comparison with the Shoah: this cartoon is titled 'Auschwitz'

'A new concentration camp'.
According to Latuff, the real Holocaust is again Palestine.
20 April 2004, cartoon presented to the Iranian Holocaust contest.

'I Am a Palestinian'. To go by Latuff's cartoons entitled 'I am a Palestinian', all persecutions from the past to the present simply foretell the martyrdom of Christ's historic people: the Palestinians. Even the little Jewish boy from the Warsaw Ghetto – the only one not to suffer ill-treatment – is... Palestinian as well (2002)

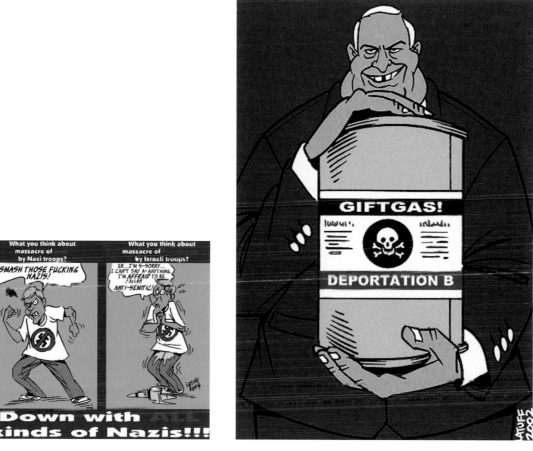

Canister of poison gas, 'Gaza Ghetto', indymedia Belgique,
8 October 2002

Not all the indymedia centres support Latuff, as witnessed here by the cartoonist's comment on the *indymedia Los Angeles* site, dated 5 February 2003: *'I feel honoured to have my cartoons very frequently reproduced in a number of Independent Media Centres, but why, you may ask, are my posters most often banned and denounced as antisemitic by German language indymedia centres? Perhaps Norman G. Finkelstein can explain.'*

Chapter 5

Anti-Zionism as a cultural code:
Israel, the scapegoat and metaphor for modernity

The intensity of the rejection of Israel cannot just be explained by the return of the repressed at the heart of a confused, guilt-ridden West, or by the solidarity implicit at street level in the Arab world with a cause it considers just and existential. This outlawing by the nations can be tracked back, in our view, to the astonishing ideological void in the present democratic left and to the function of the scapegoat allotted to the Jews ever since the Middle Ages. As we shall try to demonstrate, anti-Zionism in its extreme form is no more than the ultimate manifestation of a revolutionary or social form of anti-Judaism from the middle ages to modern times, holding the Jew chiefly responsible for all the evils in the world.

1. The left: Palestine, the new yardstick for being progressive; Israel, metaphor for capitalist evil

Palestine today emerges as one of the major unifying themes of a left that has lost its ideological direction. What other explanation can there be, at a time when it has barely recovered from the electric shock of the Le Pen factor in the French presidential election of 2002, for the decision of the Belgian Socialist Party to focus solely on the Palestinian issue in its 1 May parade, relaying messages from the Yasser Arafat's headquarters over the loudspeakers from its platform?

It is the disappearance of traditional revolutionary models which would lead to both the radical and the moderate left setting up myths about new 'resistential figures', one of which would be the Palestinian who alone epitomizes the despair of the oppressed faced with an iniquitous world order dominated by America and her ally, Israel.

This is the line taken by Pierre Galand, leading Belgian humanitarian. For this passionate activist who combines active involvement at the centre of the *Forum des peuples*, the *Amis belges du Monde diplomatique* and the Belgian-Palestinian Association, and was a socialist candidate in the Belgian election of 2003, Israel is the personification of the entire corrupt and capitalist West. Given carte blanche on the Belgian daily, *Le Soir*, to report the 'anti-racist' Forum in Durban, his writing posted *urbi et orbi* on the site of the (Maoist) Belgian Parti du Travail (PTB) confirms this attitude:

> *From their perspectives, that always reek of ultra-liberalism, the institutions of Bretton Woods (IMF, WB, WTO) are evidence of a rejection of true humanization of North-South links and exchanges. NATO regards the South as the new risk for the West and sets itself up de facto to assure the Westerners a more certain access to the riches of the South,*

whose hydrocarbons are essential to their economies. The historic dialogue organised by UNO on racism has turned into a confrontation and a door-slamming event because the North officially refutes the evidence: day by day the blacks, the Indians and so many minorities still suffer the agonies of colonialism, that have not been confronted in an honest and egalitarian fashion in accordance with the Charter of the United Nations. The rich countries of the North have never, with a few exceptions, agreed to provide the legendary one per cent of their GDP for the development of the South. There has never been an honest settling of the rates for raw materials that come from the South. In the context of magnification of deregulation and neglect of rights, Palestine has become the new Vietnam, the symbol of an unjust war. In the eyes of more and more important peoples, citizens movements, and the young, the Palestinians, a people deprived of its rights, like the Vietnamese were 50 years ago, represent a heroic and resistant South, defending its basic rights and above all its dignity in the face of an aggressive Israel, without any firm condemnation by the West. The alliance between Mr Sharon and Mr Bush, the criminal record of the former and the conservatism of the latter, constitutes a union that can only end up in international isolation of the Hebrew State and in its condemnation...[88]

In double, triple time, sliding from denunciation of capitalism in general, to Israel in particular, Pierre Galand revives the old notion of the 'Jewish financier', beloved of preachers in the times of the Crusades, and widespread ever since, especially during the nineteenth century. For this son of a 'very traditional, very Catholic and rather rich' family, as he likes to describe himself in interviews,[89] the notions of the people as Christian and the people as proletarian merge. [90]

It is advisable to link this declaration with those made by the Abbé Pierre, the other guru of the Christian left. The media star, too, repeatedly denounces the international Zionist lobby, in particular in an article originally written at the sug-gestion of *Le Monde* (who then refused to publish it), and then passed to Roger Garaudy on 28 July 1996. The pious friend of the dispossessed writes: 'The Zionist movement with its powerful leaders firmly based in the United States, and figuring strongly in every American election, is intent on possessing all the territory outlined by the Bible: from the Nile to the Euphrates. In all the political and strategic places that concern the States, the "Zionist Movement" has its secret agents, in France and elsewhere, and their doctrine emerges as more and more racist and imperialist where the Palestinians are concerned.' [91]

The struggle against Israel is a veritable crusade, permitting every kind of outrageous audacity. For this Third World militant it is quite simple: '*There is no worse violation of human rights today than the body of people who are victims of the war being conducted at present in Palestine against the Palestinian people* [sic].'[92] The hundreds of thousands of Algerian, Congolese, Kurdish, Iraqi, Chechen, Tibetan, Tutsi and Sudanese deaths are surely evidence to the contrary.

Anti-Zionism as the latest manifestation of revolutionary and/or social anti-Judaism

David Nirenberg, professor at the Johns Hopkins University in Baltimore, has explained that it was in the twelfth century that 'revolutionary anti-Judaism' appeared in the West, this strange facet of antisemitism that makes the Jew out to be the exploiter par excellence. Enslaved to sovereigns who condemned them to practise usury, the Jews were rapidly perceived as the negative symbol of royal absolute power.[93] The fact that the role of the Jews in the royal finances lasted barely a century and that the sovereigns were the sole beneficiaries (the Jews were compelled to cede back the accumulated capital) makes no odds. It is the Jews, and not the Princes (frequently as it happens claiming 'Jewishness') that are seen as evil incarnate, the enemy to be killed, that will bear the brunt of popular hatred.[94]

LE JUIF : ... BALANÇOIRES QUE TOUT ÇA

LIBERTÉ JUIVE

From the extreme right to the far left, anti-Jewish anti-capitalism flourished and culminated under the Nazis. Many were progressives that confused capitalism with Judaism, hence unleashing unbridled antisemitism. *L'Assiette au beurre* (Paris, 1907).

This medieval stereotypical image of the Jew as the 'master of finance' was to be taken up and expanded in the nineteenth century into a modern version, where the Jew becomes the incarnation of capitalism, of harsh profit and the exploitation of the proletariat.

Despite being poor in their immense majority, the Jews were rapidly considered by lazy leftists and/or those in search of a scapegoat as the symbol of the money reign. Hitherto associated with usury, the Jew was now further perceived as the prime agent of capitalist parasitism. Charles Fourier, inventor

of the phalanster, was hostile to the integration of Jews within the city.[95] His disciple, Alphonse Toussenel, went even further in his work, *Les Juifs, rois de l'époque* (1844). His slogan was '*war on the Jews*' – the enslaved populace, oppressed by capital, victims of parasitism would find emancipation only through '*the suppression of the Jews*'. For the anarchist theoretician, Pierre Proudhon, the Jew is '*the evil principle, Satan, the demon Ahriman*'. The Belgian socialist, Edmond Picard, wrote:

Let us put on the legal and socialist agenda, which is no longer a bugbear, but a vast scientific institution where keen

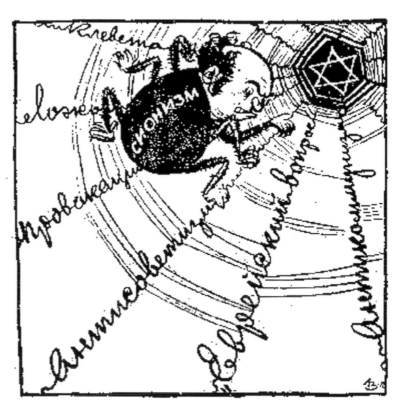

The Jew as King of Cash, *Agitator*, June 1971   The Jew spinning his web, *Sovjetskaia Moldavia*, August 1971

Soviet cartoons typifying 'revolutionary' antisemitism.

advocates of justice of all classes meet and work – ANTI-SEMITISM!

We have to consider quite objectively the suppression of Jewish influence as a security measure, and in order to achieve this, the destruction of Jewish fortunes, by introducing legislative reform of the Bourse, by repression of sterile speculation … by excluding Jews from government office…[96]

Michel Winock recalls how how in the nineteenth century certain currents of socialism admitted that antisemitism had been a preparatory programme for revolution – denouncing the Jews was, according to them, the pathway to bringing down all the bankers, and ultimately the capitalist system.

Kautsky was to hail the antisemitic movements in Hungary that in his view '*will go from strength to strength in order to deal with not only the Jews, but all the wealthy*'.[97] To paraphrase August Bebel, anti-Judaism then appeared as a form of socialism made easy. This particular form of antisemitism explains too the disgust for Jews expressed by Ulrika Meinhof, member of the Baader group: '*Auschwitz meant that six million Jews were killed and thrown on the trash heap of Europe, for being what they were: money-Jews*'.[98]

This is just the same as what is happening again today: in the same way that disgust for modern capitalism previously ended up in denunciation of the money-Jew, there are those

Two cartoons by Latuff: globalisation= capitalism=cigarettes=
McDonalds=...Israel (2002). Of course, McDonalds has nothing to
do with Israel and/or Judaism: it is not kosher.

today that connect the horrors of globalisation with Zionists.
And besides, if it is the Zionist and no longer the Jew that is
linked with the evils of capitalism, the magic formula remains
the same: anti-Zionism functioning here as the foundation for
dispute by every liberal. This is the point at which the sense of
an anti-Israeli crusade surfaces as exemplified by José Bové.

Thus, without realising it, certain third-world militants
are returning to a tradition ranging from revolutionary medieval anti-Judaism to the economic antisemitism beloved of
the trade-union anarchists of the 19th century that has always
made Israel, taken in the broadest sense, the symbol of capitalist destruction, today embodied by the United States.

2. On the far right, too, Zionism symbolises (the evils of) modernity

Obviously, the right never lagged behind on the subject of revolutionary anti-Judaism. It too made its contribution to an anti-capitalism fed on hatred and prejudice, as is always the way on the fringes of the most radical extremes of the far right.

In Europe the old antisemitism of the far right takes on a better image when supporting the Palestinian cause. And so in November 2000 Jewish community buildings in Brussels were fly-posted with small posters signed by a previously unknown,

tiny group, *Intifada européenne*. The posters showed two fedayeen in combat gear and bore the slogan *'Israel assassin!'* Superimposed was the Celtic neo-Nazi cross. The slogans of the GUD, the far right student movement founded in France in 1968, is evidence of the banality of a fiction based on paranoid anti-Zionism and anti-Americanism. *'Deauville, Sentier, occupied territories'*, *'Zionist assassins, American accomplices'*, *'Paris, like Gaza: Intifada'*, *'Not left, not right – just anti-Zionist'*.[99]

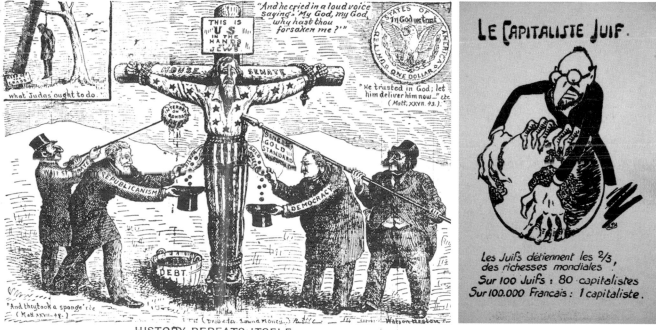

HISTORY REPEATS ITSELF.

In this American cartoon, the Jew personifies modern times – capitalist, liberal and democratic.

French fascist postcard, 1937.
'The Capitalist Jew
The Jews possess two-thirds
of the world's riches.
80 out of 100 Jews are capitalists 1 out
of 100,000 Frenchmen is a capitalist.[199bis]

Holywar.org, a far-right, antisemitic and… pro-Palestinian website

Just one example among many of the ways the Israel–Palestine conflict is being exploited by the extreme right is the website *Holywar.org*. In the name of the Palestinian cause, but also of a highly suspect anti-Zionism, this site issued in seven languages (Dutch, English, French, Italian, Norwegian, Polish, Spanish)

devotes itself whole-heartedly to criticism of the Jews. It emerges very clearly that the Palestinian cause is being used as a propaganda tool for the spiritual sons of the most extreme right wing, from the fundamentalist Catholics all the way to the neo-fascists.

Holywar.org introduces itself as a Christian resistance site, at one and the same time '100% anti-Nazi, 100% anti-Zionist, 100% anti-Communist and 100% anti-hate.'

'The Satanic Jewish symphony brings nothing but death. Act before it is too late. Holy war.'

A call to Christians to fight against the Jewish domination of America (see the flag).
Holywar.org, Norwegian page.

www.holywar.org, 2002–03

www.holywar.org, 2002–03

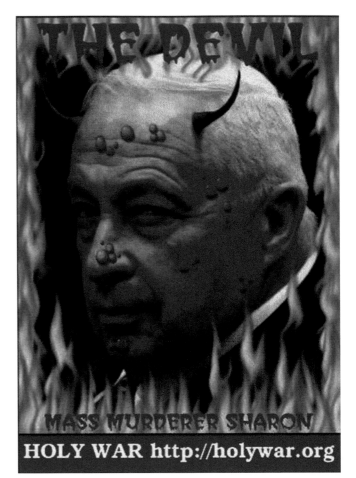

'The Devil. Sharon, mass criminal'. Holywar.com do not hesitate to reproduce this Latuff cartoon. They share the same hatred.
Latuff, *www.holywar.org*, 2002–03

The Jewish Mafia runs America and Ukraine

President Bush waves on the way to JEWISH TALMUD CLASS, accompanied by his former White House press secretary and newly ordained JEWISH RABBI Ari Fleischer. Sources have confirmed that PRESIDENT OF THE UNITED STATES G.W. BUSH IS REALLY A CRYPTO-ZIONIST JEW.
Stop the Zionist plot against America. Politicians are only puppets, the real power lies with the Zionist Jews, who hide behind the puppet politicians. Help us expose them to the public.

Everyone who is not a pure fascist is Jewish, from Yushchenko to Berlusconi.
Berlusconi with a kippah... 'the marrano (closet Jew) forgets the 9,000 Palestinian innocent victims of Jewish oppression...'

www.holywar.org, 2002–03

The Devil (Benedict XVI) and the Good Lord(s) Ahmadinedjad and Chávez. The Iranian President is the new icon of the extreme right: because he proclaims he want to finish Hitler's job?

People all over the world are taking ACTION because for the first time in their life they can see clearly that the racist Jew is responsible for bringing the international community into worldwide conflict and the disastrous consequences that will surely follow. It is because of the racist Jew and the current United States regime's unconditional support of the Satanic Jewish Israeli state... despite the atrocities that Israeli commits against it's neighboring countries that has brought to U.S. soil the reality of a very unsure future, a future in which American citizenry will never know where or when the next terrorist act will occur on American soil.

FIGHT THE RACIST JEWISH MAFIA!

HOLY WAR - http://holywar.org

www.holywar.org, 2002–03

KOMMUNISMEN = KAPITALISMEN = SIONISMEN. BEKJEMP DEM !

FRIGJØR UNIVERSITETET FRA AKP-FASCISMEN !

 FOLKETS MOTSTANDSBEVEGELSE (Det Kristne Alternativet!)
http://holywar.org

'Communism=capitalism=Zionism... Fight them! Liberate the university from fascism. AKP!'
www.holywar.org, 2002–03

The only two real (Jewish) holocausts:
Abortion (against the Christians) and Genocide (against the Palestinians)

Most of the neo-Nazi movements support the Palestinian cause – much to the displeasure of Carlos Latuff, who ought to be well aware that since the nineteenth century the ultra-radical far right and the ultra-radical far right are agreed in the area of radical anti-Zionism.
(n.d.)

Cover of a classic
publication by the pro-life movement.
The name of the Jewish abortionist doctor is
symptomatic: Dr Herod.
Here we have a contemporary echo of the myth of the Massacre
of the Innocents (note the shooting star and the three camels of
the Magi in the background) (n.d.)[100]

Denouncing abortion and 'the aborters' is a modern version of the myth of the Jew as a child murderer. The pro-life movements are now exploiting the words 'holocaust' and 'genocide' (see above) in no way alluding to the Shoah but to the millions of infant victims of the Jewish Abortion Industry as well as to the Palestinian victims of Zionism.

3. At the heart of the Arab world too: Israel, the metaphor for modernity

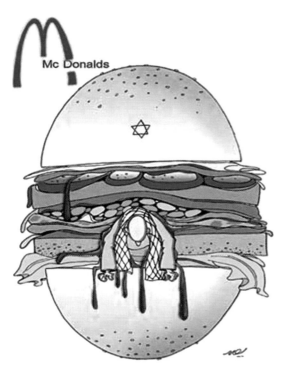

Mehdi Sadegh (Iran), n.d.

'American hamburger', al Quds
(Palestine), 9 September 2001

Arabia.com, 2002
Three 'progressive' cartoons denouncing the Zionist hamburger

At the heart of the Arab-Muslim world the confusion between 'Zionism' and 'Americanisation of the world' is reaching new heights, by a process that is incomprehensible, if one loses sight of the function of the scapegoat historically allotted to the Jews, including in the centre of the Arab world. When a major crisis arises, such as the one currently spreading across the Muslim world, once again the explanation is attributed to the Jew and by association to the American as the prime source of evil.

Denounced as capitalists, the Jews are inevitably associated with the most disastrous aspects of modernity. Vast numbers of people from Morocco to Pakistan, to the suburbs of Paris and London consider that certain products widely distributed in the consumer society (such as Marlboro, Coca Cola, McDonalds, etc.) are if not Zionist then at least anti-Muslim. This applies to Procter and Gamble's Ariel washing powder, suspected of promoting Ariel... Sharon.[101] According to several political movements with Islamic allegiance, Ariel, in fact 'bears the name of the Israeli Prime Minister and displays a logo representing the Star of David, symbol of the Jew-

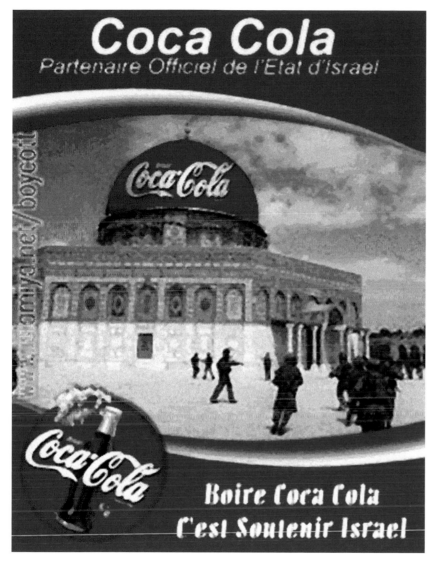

THIS IS THE COCA COLA LOGO.

IF WE FLIP IT HORIZONTALY, IT WOULD LOOK LIKE THIS, RIGHT?

NOW WATCH CAREFULLY AS THE IMAGE IS ADJUSTED

IF YOU CAN READ ANY ARABIC, YOU CAN TELL WHAT IT SAYS.

(La Mohammed, La Mecca)

WHICH MEANS:

NO MOHAMMAD
NO MAKKAH

To all you Muslims out there, this drink has a KAFIR statement on it yet you still drink it! You still buy it!

SPREAD THIS OUT TO THE ENTIRE UMMAH

'Drink Coca Cola, it supports Israel...'[18]   *'Let the entire Muslim community know.'*[17]

ish people.'[102] Procter and Gamble, giant manufacturer of products with major distribution, did not take the boycott threats seriously until figures revealed a substantial drop in the sales of Ariel. The press release issued by the management of the multinational explaining that *'Ariel washing powder existed long before the Prime Minister of Israel (1920) and that the logo in fact symbolised the trajectory of atoms in fabric'* did not convince Egyptian and Palestinian housewives. Sales of Ariel have virtually ceased here and there. All American brands have fallen victim to this confusion. It is particularly the case with McDonalds, the leading example of American modernity and bizarrely linked with Israel and Zionism. McDonalds was, in fact, only set up in Israel fairly recently, as its products are not kosher.

Coca Cola is another instance of this kind of confusion. In order to maintain competition, the American brand has put into production *Zamzam Cola* (Iran), *Mecca Cola* (France/Tunisia), militant fizzy drinks 10% of whose profits supposedly go towards social work all over the world, particularly Palestinian and Muslim.

There is absolutely nothing whatsoever to link the firm of Atlanta with the Jewish world. Just as, moreover, there is no connection between the Jews and the Japanese Pokemon. And yet… There again allegations and denunciations have been gathering force.

Pokemon as a 'Zionist conspiracy'

When the Pokemon, those grimacing little monsters printed on playing cards suddenly burst on to the scene, they soon raised alarm among the religious authorities in the Arab countries, not only in Saudi Arabia, in Qatar, in Dubai, where the game was prohibited, but also in Jordan, where there was instant suspicion of some Zionist

www.arabia.com/jordan/hajjaj/

Here the cartoonist Hajjaj ridicules the futility of the Arab boycott of Pokemon.

plot hidden behind those drawings created by some honest Japanese citizen. A former Islamic deputy of the Hashemite parliament, Sheikh Abden Moneim Abu Zant, did not hesitate to attribute the paternity of the Pokemon to 'the Zionist entity'. *'This Pokemon epidemic is a Jewish plot aimed at forcing our children to forget their faith and distract them from their scientific ambitions.'* The sheikh concluded by saying: *'This game is an offence against God, and must be banned.'*

That is how the Jordanian religious authorities came to order them *'all to be caught'*. The spread of the game also raised some concern in the Christian community of Amman. In April 2001 Father Emmanuel Estephan Banna, of the Syrian Orthodox community, received some anonymous messages claiming that *'the word Pokemon and the names of the characters in this game are Jewish and are of Syriac origin; they are an insult to Islam.'* If these messages are to be believed, Pokemon would mean *'I am Jewish'* in Japanese according to some, and to others in Syriac, and Pikashu (the hero of Pokemon) would be *'an offensive description of Allah (God)'*. The highest religious authorities of the Syrian Church in Jerusalem exploded in indignation. Father Emmanuel issued a statement in the national press, denying any connection between his community and the little monsters. Does *Pokemon* mean 'Jew' in Japanese? The Japanese cultural attaché in Amman, Koji Tahara, received numerous requests for elucidation on the subject. *'Jew in the language of the Empire of the Rising Sun is pronounced "Youdayajin" which is not really close to "Pokemon"'* was the diplomat's reply, and saw fit to add *'"Pokemon" is a contraction of "pocket monsters".'*[103]

In his *fatwah* of 24 March 2001, the Mufti of Saudi Arabia had recommended *'all Muslims to distrust this game and prevent their children from playing it in order to preserve their religion and their manners.*[104] The Dubai *fatwah* went even further, asserting that *'the Pokemon were based on the theory of evolution, a Judaeo-Darwinian theory in opposition to the truth and the principles of Islam.'*[105] A month later the Palestinian religious authorities in their turn called for a boycott of the Pokemon in the territories under Palestinian authority, under the pretext that Pikashu and his friends looked 'suspiciously Jewish'.[106]

Tom and Jerry a 'Jewish conspiracy'

Professor Hasan Bulkhari, a senior cultural adviser to Iran's Education Ministry, recently stated that the animated series 'Tom and Jerry' was created as part of a Jewish conspiracy. Bulkhari explained that the cartoon aimed at shifting the image of mice – often attributed to Jews by the Nazi regime – from a negative one to a more positive, friendly, intelligent one, according to Worldnetdaily. Speaking on a televised programme on Iranian television, the advisor explained, 'The mouse is the wise and smart one, and he violently beats the poor cat. And yet, this cruelty does not cause you to despise the mouse. He looks so nice, and he is smart.' 'The Jews were degraded and termed "dirty mice". "Tom and Jerry" was made in order to change the Europeans' perception of mice. One of terms used was "dirty mice".' 'It should be noted that mice are very cunning ... and dirty.' 'The program was produced in an attempt to erase the image of the mouse from the minds of European children and to show that the mouse is not dirty and that he even has nice characteristics,' he pointed out. 'The Jewish Walt Disney Company gained international fame with this cartoon,' he said. 'If you study European history, you will see who was the main power in hoarding money and wealth in the nineteenth century,' continued Bulkhari. 'In most cases, it is the Jews. Perhaps that was one of the reasons which caused Hitler to begin the anti-Semitic trend, and then the extensive propaganda about the crematoria began... Some of this is true. We do not deny all of it.'[107]

The Muslim paranoia towards the Jews has no limit. Let us remember that Tom and Jerry were created in 1939 by Hanna and Barbera and not by Walt Disney, very often denounced as a Jew.[108] The fact that he was not Jewish or – according to certain absurd rumours – an antisemite, has no importance. The comic strip industry is modern, so, as such... Jewish.

Tehran, February 2006. Demonstration against Muhammad cartoons. One interesting feature of the demonstrations is how often Israel, which had nothing to do with the cartoon 'issue' is attacked.

4. Israel, the scapegoat

They left Paris, taking the road for Aquitaine. They killed all the Jews they met here and there, and stripped them of their belongings. 'Why the Jews?' I asked Salvatore. He replied, 'And why not?' And then he explained to me that all their lives they had learned from the mouths of the preachers that the Jews were the enemies of Christianity, and amassed all the goods that they themselves were denied. I asked him whether it wasn't however the goods that were amassed by the lords and the bishops from their tithes and that the shepherd boys weren't fighting against their real enemies. He replied by saying that you need to choose the weakest as your enemies, as the real enemies are always too strong. I asked who it was that had put it into the heads of all these people that they should attack the Jews. Salvatore couldn't remember.

Umberto Eco, *The Name of the Rose*

The capacity to identify a scapegoat is, according to René Girard, one of the primordial components of Western culture. In his *La violence et le sacré* the French philosopher showed that violent unanimity is a universal mechanism in conflict resolution, a spontaneous means of escaping from the Hobbesian nightmare of war by all against all. The individuals on whom the community unloads all its violence are then accused of the most horrendous crimes, of transgression or even of the desire to abolish the prohibitions established by all societies. Only by getting rid of them can the cultural and social differences that constitute society be restored – differences between the sexes, the generations, the social hierarchies, the distinction between that which is internal and that which is external to a community, etc. Myth tells of an expulsion or a collective murder, that religious ritual par

excellence is intended to replicate, to mime, according to very precise regulations, in order to preserve order and peace within the community. In comparing the structures of myths the world over, there is one recurrent theme that is always present, more or less concealed by the account – the murder or collective expulsion of an individual, identified as a god or a hero, a marginal figure or a monster, whose 'appearance' has aroused violence and whose disappearance will restore peace to the community.[109] Now, as proposed by Yves Chevalier in his thesis presented at the Sorbonne in 1986, it is precisely the Jews who have fulfilled this very particular role in the West, on account both of the mistrust they inspire in Christians and the eminently religious character of Judaism as seen by those same Christians.[110] In order to restore harmony and social peace, to calm and reassure the people, all that is necessary from time to time is to take it out on the Jews (physical attack, conversion, expulsion, killing etc.) Philippe-Auguste, Philippe the Fair, and Charles VIII all earned the love and the trust of the people by this means. The 'Jew' enabled Evil to be identified and at the same time showed that this same evil could be defeated.

Greater Israel in relation to France – Israel is 768 times smaller than the United States. It is two-thirds the size of Belgium, or 45% the extent of the French département of Aquitaine (20,770 sq. km). Israel's strength appears all the greater since it is almost invisible.

5. Israel – the nations' Jew

The favoured status linking Israel and the United States applies mostly to the area affected by anti-Zionism. In a universe whose predominant feature is hostility towards the United States, opposition to Israel seems like a convenient and easy way of opposing the current leader. Looking at Girard's thesis, this attitude is all the more attractive because the Jewish state is not a real power. Contrary to the selective imagery by which it is portrayed, this country is, in fact, a state of very modest significance – six million inhabitants, a GDP per head comparable to that of Spain and covering an area smaller than Belgium. Europe is better off lashing out head-on against Israel, the nations' Jew, and against Sharon, than attacking China's Tiananmen Square, Russia's dirty war against Chechnya or Saudi Arabia's al-Qaeda.[111]

All it needs is to portray this country, Israel, as what it is not – a superpower. By so doing it becomes if not the true *master of the world game* then certainly the equal of the United States, of the USSR, if not China (and others). An interpretation that leads a certain Jean-Paul Lewidoff of Paris, in a letter to the editor of *Le Monde* on 30 October 2002, to expose the true root of contemporary evil: *'Should we not ask ourselves in these initial years of the twenty-first century whether the rogue states are not in fact the United States, Russia and Israel (sic)? Today it is these hyper-armed states, the United States, Russia and Israel that generate and sustain world disorder.'*

The scapegoat must never appear as what it really is – a defenceless animal, destined at best to be hunted, at worst for sacrifice – but as what it is not, harmful and super-powerful. The advantage of this deceit is to be able to disguise a simple, vague desire for sacrifice as a noble and difficult combat. This subconscious style based on the fantasy of Jewish power, explains the tremendous resurgence of judeophobia in progressive circles and the ease with which this feeling has been

Abdala Mahraqy, *akhbar-alkhaleej* (Bahrain), 16 September 2006
For this cartoonist the Jews must be behind the Pope's declaration

Abdala Mahraqy, *akhbar-alkhaleej* (Bahrain) 17 September 2006

Abdala Mahraqy, *akhbar-alkhaleej* (Bahrain), 18 September 2006

This cartoon by the Australian Michael Leunig has been posted both on extreme left sites (*Indymedia*) as well as on sites of the far right (*Jewish-tribalreview.org*)

planted in supposedly liberal minds. In just the same way that in the Middle Ages attacking Jews was a way of gaining approval from the sovereign in power, the present trend is to identify Israel as responsible for the ills of the world, if not as Evil itself. From now on it all comes from the non-resolution of the Israeli–Palestinian conflict – the attack on 11 September, al-Qaeda, the Bali massacre or the Iraqi crisis. It's tempting to say that if Israel didn't exist they would have to invent

her! This is the meaning of the editorial signed by Philippe Val, editor in chief of *Charlie Hebdo*, on 3 April 2002:

So you're looking for a reason? Simple! Israel versus Palestine, it's the World Trade Organisation versus Porto Alegre. The Jewish and Palestinian people are being made into symbols of a political conflict that threatens to engulf them. They are being sacrificed on the altar of the simplification of international opinion...

Sharon is a product of Arafat who has always harboured a terrorist movement, the desperate are a product of Sharon, and at this time, there we are like idiots making Arafat an icon of world discussion. The fact that the Sri Lankans are bleeding to death by the hundreds of thousands, no one gives a damn. There isn't even any attempt to discover who is in the right and who in the wrong. Why hasn't Bové been to Tibet, and put himself between the army and the monks? Because Tibet is not the symbolic friction point between the American zone of influence and the Third World, which we like to think is resisting it.

We are a long way from defending the rights of the Palestinians. We are guilty of being foolish enough to introduce a cause into the argument – that of the ecological and social future of the planet – that makes heroes of the ones and disqualifies the others, for reasons that derive from a media interpretation that makes no great attempt to look into the true aspirations of the peoples concerned. But – what can you do – anti-globalisation sells papers, which hasn't escaped the notice of those in the lead of anti-globalisation. Today the entire French press and media supports

A veiled Muslim protester, holding a placard, marches towards the Danish embassy during a demonstration in London, Friday Feb. 3, 2006 (AP Photo/Lefteris Pitarakis).

Arafat, a bit like José Bové was supported when he stood up for Roquefort cheese. Arafat is one of those elements responsible for the duration of a system based on 'the consumption of fast thinking' along the lines of 'fast food'.

For the nth time in its history Israel again finds itself in the position of the tailor-made guilty party, with some going so far as to suggest that it should once and for all be sacrificed to the Beast. In the words of Pierre-André Taguieff: '*The fundamental implicit argument may be rephrased:* 'If Israel didn't exist, peace and justice would reign in the Middle East', *in addition to which there is the subsidiary argument whereby Islamic terrorism would no longer have, as a result of this non-existence, any justification or reasons for existing (which presupposes that it has reasons for existing at present!). The practical and stated reason for such an argument can thus be succinctly put: 'Israel is a surplus country and must disappear.*[112]

The new anti-Zionism, as we have said only too often, does not see Israel as a state like any other; on the contrary, its assumption is that the world would be a better place if this country did not exist.

Epilogue

'Peace is not an absence of war, it is a virtue, a state of mind, a disposition for benevolence, confidence, justice.'
Spinoza

Hate culture or peace culture?

The aim of our study, apart from denouncing an editorial practice that is the source of hatred and incomprehension, is therefore to alert the cartoonists of the Arab-Muslim region to a certain sense of responsibility. To point the finger at a leader, to put a policy on trial is one thing; to accuse an entire people is another. For information we reprint the list of journalistic failings denounced and enumerated in his time by one of the fathers of research into peace (*Peace Studies and Conflict Resolution*), the Norwegian Johan Galtung. It clearly demonstrates what cartoonists and other polemicists should stop doing, in so far of course that they intend to promote the cause of peace and justice, and not that of war and hatred. He laid out 12 points of concern where journalism often goes wrong when dealing with violence. Each implicitly suggests more explicit remedies.

1. Decontextualising violence: focusing on the irrational without looking at the reasons for unresolved conflicts and polarisation.

2. Dualism: reducing the number of parties in a conflict to two, when often more are involved. Stories that just focus on internal developments often ignore such outside or 'external' forces as foreign governments and transnational companies.

3. Manichaeism: portraying one side as good and demonising the other as 'evil'.

4. Armageddon: presenting violence as inevitable, omitting alternatives.

5. Focusing on individual acts of violence while avoiding structural causes, like poverty, government neglect and military or police repression.

6. Confusion: focusing only on the conflict arena (i.e., the battlefield or location of violent incidents) but not on the forces and factors that influence the violence.

7. Excluding and omitting the bereaved, thus never explaining why there are acts of revenge and spirals of violence.

8. Failure to explore the causes of escalation and the impact of media coverage itself.

9. Failure to explore the goals of outside interventionists, especially major powers.

10. Failure to explore peace proposals and offer images of peaceful outcomes.

11. Confusing ceasefires and negotiations with actual peace.

12. Omitting reconciliation: conflicts tend to re-emerge if attention is not paid to efforts to heal fractured societies. When news about attempts to resolve conflicts is absent, fatalism is reinforced. That can help engender even more violence, when people have no images or information about possible peaceful outcomes and the promise of healing.

All criticism is permissible, but not by any means whatever

We want to make it plain – we are in no way trying to compel Arab and European cartoonists to morph into keen champions of the State of Israel. That would make no sense. But is it too much to ask them to refrain from playing on collective fears, as they are doing on an everyday basis, at the risk of creating unbridgeable gulfs and permanent antagonism? The comments and the images they juggle can only promote hatred, absolute hatred of Israel *and* of the Jews, in short poisoning for all time a conflict that is already extremely complex. The activities of the media – and we have the Rwandan example to remind us – can lead to genocide.

Youngsters less than 15 years old constitute the vast majority of the population of the Arab countries. Now all that they know about the Jewish and Israeli reality is what the press of their country and their school text books give them to feed on – images of another age. The fact that these images are fantasies, makes no difference. How much does reality count for in the face of rumour and lies? Alfred Grosser has isolated one of the central points of political analysis when he emphasised the importance of the image and perception: *'It is constantly necessary to be aware of the two orders of reality. On the one hand there is the material fact, that can be isolated and described, on the other hand the representations that participants in the political game have of this fact. This representation, this belief creates in its turn a fact that is often more important for its consequences than the original fact.'*[114]

That blood is forbidden to Jews, even when it comes from kosher animals, is of little significance if the masses have been convinced to the contrary. How can we forget that the 1930s spawned evil images of the Jew in France and in Germany, to which the French and the Germans became so accustomed that to a large extent this explains the ease with which they carried out the Shoah?

However there are some nuances that must be observed. There is no question of denouncing as antisemitic, or indeed anti-Zionist these few anti-Israeli cartoons that we have reprinted here. It makes no difference whether or not we share the opinions put forward by the cartoonists. By including these examples, we wish to demonstrate that it is possible to stand up for certain ideas – and in so doing to criticise a state, a policy, a head of state – without demonising the enemy.

T. Mughal (Dpa), 15 February 2006
Islamic rally in Pakistan

Appendix 1

It is possible to criticise Israel without giving way to antisemitism. Here are some examples.

Chapatte, *Le Temps*, Switzerland, n.d.

Plantu, *Le Monde*, France, 6–7 June 1991

Heng, *Zao Boa*, Singapore, n.d.

Ique, *Jornal Do Brazil*, Brazil, n.d.

Appendix 2
Some unacceptable anti-Palestinian cartoons

However, whereas the cartoons in the Israeli press are not usually racist, nonetheless the occasional anti-Arab examples do crop up here and there. Among these are the cartoons by Oleg, an Israeli artist of Russian origin and advocate of Greater Israel. Likewise the photomontages of *Kach*, the racist movement prohibited in Israel, but firmly rooted in the United States. As is evident from the examples that follow, they are quite brutal, if not vulgar. They take on the Palestinian Authority and the Israeli government with equal fervour. Itzhak Rabin and Shimon Peres were their pet hates. Sharon is today! And how. The fact remains that however unpleasant they may be, they are in no way typical of Israeli press cartoons. They are and remain confidential. *Kach*, that issues the photomontages reproduced here, is actually banned in Israel.

Three examples of zoomorphisation:
Kach (1 and 2) and Oleg (3)

Church of the Nativity

Consistently disgraceful:
left, cartoon by Oleg; right, photomontage from *Kach*

Cartoon by Oleg against the Oslo Accords

Appendix 3
The usual suspects: the Jews behind the Muhammad Cartoons

The Muhammad Cartoon Is a Jewish Attempt to Divert European Hatred from Jews to Muslims

Al-Qardaghi: *We must realise that something bigger than this [cartoon] incident lies behind this campaign. The Zionists and the Christian far right are behind it – not all (the) Christians. Honourable brothers, a survey conducted some time ago in Europe showed that 67% of Europeans hate the Jews. The Jewish leaders convened to decide what to do. They wanted to divert this hatred to the Muslims. This is a Crusader Zionist campaign, which is led by the extremist pro-Zionist right, headed by George Bush in America. I am sad to say this. This campaign is an attempt to arouse religious, Crusader fanaticism among the European peoples, because they were not responsive to the extremist right. They want to do so by provoking the Muslims, and perhaps by some inappropriate deeds.*

[...]

Brothers, the person who lit the fuse was a Jew from Denmark. He wrote a book called The Koran and the Life of Muhammad, in which he claimed that the Prophet Muhammad was the first Nazi, and that he carried out the first Jewish holocaust. He said that the killing of the Jews in Al-Madina was a holocaust. They distorted everything. Then he asked a hundred artists to illustrate it, but they refused, so he approached this pro-Zionist newspaper, which agreed. The Zionists, Jews, and Crusaders are behind this issue.

Excerpts from an address by Qatari university lecturer Ali Muhi Al-Din Al-Qardaghi, broadcast on Al-Jazeera TV, 3 February 2006.

1. The Muhammad cartoon affair

The *Jyllands-Posten* Muhammad cartoons controversy began after twelve editorial cartoons, most of which depicted the Islamic prophet Muhammad, were published in the Danish newspaper *Jyllands-Posten* on 30 September 2005. The newspaper explained that this publication was a contribution to the debate over criticism of Islam and self-censorship. In response, Danish Muslim organisations held public protests and publicised the contents of *Jyllands-Posten*'s issue. In the beginning, the Muhammad cartoons controversy attracted relatively little media attention outside Denmark. Six of the cartoons were even reprinted by the Egyptian newspaper *El Fagr* on 17 October 2005 along with an article strongly denouncing them, but the publication did not provoke any condemnations

or other reactions from religious or government authorities. Between October 2005 and the end of January 2006, examples of the cartoons were reprinted in major European newspapers from the Netherlands, Germany, Scandinavia, Belgium and France.

In December 2005, a group of Danish imams, dissatisfied with the reaction of the Danish government and *Jyllands-Posten*, set out for a tour of the Middle East to present their case to many influential religious and political

177

Françoise Pichard, alias Chard, regularly draws cartoons for the daily Présent and the weekly Rivarol, two extreme-right publications connected to the Jean-Marie Le Pen's National Front.

A non-caricatural view of the Danish affair seen by a young and brilliant Canadian artist, J..J. McCullough

leaders, and ask for support. These Danish imams produced a 43-page document entitled *Dossier about championing the prophet Muhammad, peace be upon him*. The dossier consists of several letters from Muslim organisations explaining their case, citing the *Jyllands-Posten* cartoons but also the following causes of 'pain and torment' to the authors:

1. Pictures from another Danish newspaper, *Weekendavisen*, which they called '*even more offensive*' (than the original twelve cartoons);
2. Hate-mail pictures and letters that the dossier's authors alleged were sent to Muslims in Denmark, said to be indicative of the rejection of Muslims by the Danes;
3. A televised interview discussing Islam with the Dutch member of parliament and Islam critic Hirsi Ali, who had received the Freedom Prize '*for her work to further freedom of speech and the rights of women*' by the Danish Liberal Party represented by Anders Fogh Rasmussen.

Appended to the dossier were multiple clippings from *Jyllands-Posten*, from *Weekendavisen*, some clippings from Arabic-language papers, and three additional images. The first image was later found to be a press photo of a contestant at a French pig-squealing contest; the second portrayed a Muslim being mounted by a dog while praying and the third portrayed Muhammad as a demonic paedophile. At the summit of the Organisation of the Islamic Conference held on 6 December 2005, with many heads of state in attendance, the dossier was passed around, unofficially at first, and eventually an official communiqué was issued, demanding that the United Nations impose international sanctions upon Denmark.

As the controversy grew, examples of the cartoons were reprinted in newspapers in more than fifty other countries, which led to violent protests, including rioting especially in the Muslim world.

Critics of the cartoons describe them as 'Islamophobic' and/or argue that they are blasphemous for people of the Muslim faith, intended to humiliate a marginalised Danish minority, in a context of rising intolerance in Denmark, and are a manifestation of ignorance of the history of Western imperialism, from colonialism to the current conflicts in the Middle East.

Supporters of the cartoons claim they illustrate an important issue in a period of Islamic extremist terrorism and that their publication is a legitimate exercise of freedom of speech. They also claim that similar cartoons about other religions are frequently printed, arguing that the followers of Islam were not targeted in a discriminatory way. Danish Prime Minister Anders Fogh Rasmussen described the controversy as Denmark's worst international crisis since the Second World War.

Our intention is not to enter into this debate. In our view, most of the Danish cartoons except for one are quite mediocre. Furthermore, one of them could really be seen as blasphemous to Islam. Should they have been forbidden? Certainly not! A democratic state cannot permit censorship of its artists: freedom of the press and of opinion (unless racist) is not negotiable. Should they have been published? Absolutely not! Renouncement of any notion of censorship doesn't mean renouncement of any idea of limit. There must be limits, even in cartoons, but they should only be set by the profession itself or by tribunals, in the case of libel. It is solely up to the cartoonists and/or the editor to judge whether a drawing really is a caricature, i.e. a possibly extreme exaggeration of the truth, or a totally false and slanderous representation, that contributes nothing to the debate or may even inflame it. So, if an artist can make fun of a religion such as Islam, even in an exaggerated way – this is the prerogative of the professional – he cannot do so by making his pencil lie. Islam as such is not a religion that promotes terrorism.

Our point is different. It is to stress the absurdity of the fact that many Arab intellectuals detected a Jewish hand behind the scenes. Why? Because of the strange and now commonplace habit of attributing responsibility for all Arab misfortunes to the Jews!

2. The Arab response: the Jews must be guilty!

Abdala Mahraqi, *Akhbar-Alkhaleej* (Bahrain),
1 February 2006

Flag in cheese: 'Danish Product Boycott It'
On right: 'The Penetration of Zionism to Denmark'
Abdala Mahraqi, *Akhbar al-Khalij (Bahrain)*, 29 January 2006.
In Danish cheese, you've also got worms.

Mwafaq Farazat, *Al Watan* (Saudi Arabia),
11 February 2006

Fares Garabet (Syria), *Al Raya* (Qatar), 8 February 2006
What they do with historians that deny the Holocaust!

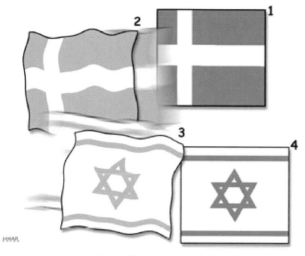

Tarek Bahar, *Akhbar-Alkhaleej* (Bahrain), 8 February 2006

Kamal Sulman (Syria), *A Shahed* magazine,
second week of February 2006

Khaled Kataa (Syria), February 2006

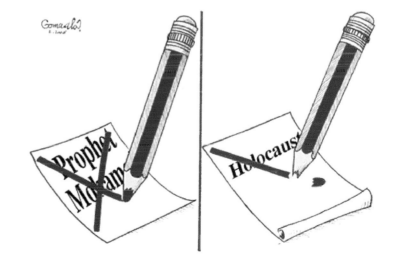

Translation: 'The Western Media',
Al-Watan (Saudi Arabia), 11 February

The tragic certitudes of Ismail Mohammed Effat, president of FECO Egypt.

For Ismail Mohammed Effat, the president of the Egyptian section of the *Federation of Cartoonists' Organisations* (FECO) there is absolutely no doubt that the hand of the Jew lies hidden behind the Danish scene. In his inimitably naïve manner, he does not hesitate to identify the Jewish guilt in two separate issues of his bulletin *Pharaohs* (nos. 35 and 36). He goes even further by reproducing anti-Zionist/antisemitic drawings made by deaf children. Apparently sure of what he defends, he even doesn't hesitate to address open letters to his European collegues, in particular to Marlene Pohle, the German President of FECO and to its Secretary General, the Dutchman Peter Nieuwendijk. That M. Effat draws antisemitic cartoons mostly out of ignorance is bad enough; but that he is still the representative of FECO in Egypt is far worse. For FECO with its world-wide membership of over 2,000 artists from 30 countries, to remain silent, is tragic. Has Marlene Pohl forgotten the damage done by *Der Stürmer*?

مجلة كاريكاتورية تصدر بالقاهرة عن اتحاد منظمات رسامي الكاريكاتير (فيكو) بمصر
Cartoon Magazine Published in Cairo by F E C O - Egypt

Issue 35 – February 2005   العدد ٣٥ - فبراير ٢٠٠٦م

No .. Prophet's Carticature !!
لا .. لرسومات الأنبياء

ي هذا العدد سنتعرض لما دار من
راسلات حول موضوع نشر بعض
لرسامين من الدنمرك لرسومات تمس
لخصية الرسول سيدنا محمد (صلى الله
عليه وسلم). واعتراضنا ورفضنا
سلمين وكعرب وكإدارة المجلة أيضا
ن موقف هؤلاء الرسامين.

In this issue we'll discuss ir what happen in som correspondence around th twelve cartoons published b some cartoonists fron Denmark which insult Prophe Mohamed (God's blessing and peace be upon him). And we a Moslems, Arabs, and also, a board of Pharaohs magazine condemns this caricatures

**General Supervisor:
Mohamed Effat Ismail
*President FECO of EGYPT***
Tel.: (202) 2058383
effatcartoon@hotmail.com
Address:10 Menitte El-Serege St.,
Shoubra - Garden, 11241
Cairo - Egypt

Dear Esmail,
I have just seen some of your 'work' on the internet and let me tell you that you are not good at what you do. The fact that you have completed many years of education and got many awards don't matter. Your awards had political motives behind them, but your so called 'art' speaks for itself. They are not funny, and you keep torturing the already tortured to death 'Jews versus Arabs' subject. May be this is the right time for you to rethink your life.
kurabaya@hotmail.com

Thank you your respect mail, but this your opinion only, and it's not very important for me!!

Effat 'President of FECO Egypt'

By: EFFAT
Dear friend Marlene Pohle
FECO President
Peter Nieuwendijk
FECO Secretary General

Thank you for your message about Sayidena 'Mohamed' (Salaa ALLAH Alieh Wa Sallm), and I would like to explain some point in our religion as: In our religion: The God is one for all the people, and the God send for the people all prophets from 'Sayidena Nouh' until Sayidena 'Mohamed' (Salaa ALLAH Alieh Wa Sallm).Also, all prophets were from Sayidena 'Ibrahim' progeny, and all Muslim believes in all prophets, and no difference between them. So, it's deep deferent between the Joke (by Caricature) about any persons (like: Presidents, General Persons, Stars, players… etc) there is no problem!! But, Joke about any prophets it's impossible and prohibited in our religion. Although, in the West Culture is permissible to use cartoons about 'Christ'!! but in the East Culture we respect all prophets, (Sayidena Ibrahim, Sayidena Essaa 'Christ', Sayidena Mosaa and Sayidena 'Mohamed' (Salaa ALLAH Alieh Wa Sallm) the last of prophets. About your opinion about 'bearded', you're sure and know that in all world there is 'bearded' not in Moslem only, but there are in the Jews, and the Christian bearded people. At least, are there any cartoonist drawing about HOLOCAUST!!! And now we needed dialogue between East and West Culture by cartoons.

Sultan El Sebay – Arab Saudi

الفراعنة
Pharaohs

مجلة كاريكاتورية تصدر بالقاهرة عن اتحاد منظمات رسامي الكاريكاتير (فيكو) بمصر
Cartoon Magazine Published in Cairo by F E C O - Egypt

Issue 36 – March 2006　　العدد ٣٦ - مارس ٢٠٠٦م

Denmark's attack on Egypt
Embassador in Copenhagen　　هجوم دانمركي على سفيرة مصر في كوبنهاجن!

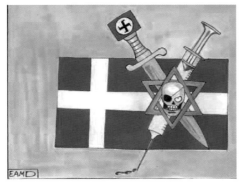

Emad Ahmed Mohamed Mosaa

Issue 36 - Page 3

AGAIN MAKE HUMOUR NOT WAR !!

So I think that the Danish attack on our prophet Mohamed and the other prophets need in return for it a quake. And we all know that the journal whom had published the caricatures against prophet Mohamed and Jesus Christ put the symbol of Star of David in the head of the first page. So the Danish caricaturist must know that :

The caricature =
the pleasure + politeness

And the politeness here is respecting prophets, respecting the affairs of Palestinians, dealing with fair with the affair of Holocaust (it's victims from Jews was little) or the Holocaust is just using it to mislead the mass media to forget the problem of the Palestine's people. At last we must know that love is pleasure but first we must know what love means and unfortunately we didn't know what it mean yet. And the caricaturist is a prophet with a philosophical opinion.

So what is the pleasure of the good caricature??

It's 2 kind :

•The first one is a caricature of soul and mind and this one remain with our soul and mind and it will never vanish.

•The second one of being and emotions and this one is superficial live on the instincts of body and it vanish by the vanishing of the body and the emotions.

Effat
"President of FECO Egypt"

الجمعية الأهلية للصم
NATIONAL ASSOCIATION OF THE DEAF
مشهرة برقم ٣٦٧ لسنة ١٩٩٧

Education School nature cartoons
in National Association of the Deaf (Egypt)　　مدرسة تعليم الكاريكاتير الفطري
بالجمعية الأهلية للصم بمصر

Hanan El-Nahrawy
effatcartoon@hotmail.com

Hany Mohamed Mohamed El-Sagher
effatcartoon@hotmail.com

Mohamed Mousbah Shaaban
effatcartoon@hotmail.com

Education School nature cartoons
in National Association of the Deaf (Egypt)　　مدرسة تعليم الكاريكاتير الفطري
بالجمعية الأهلية للصم بمصر

Emad Ahmed Mohamed Mosaa effatcartoon@hotmail.com

Hany Mohamed Samir
effatcartoon@hotmail.com

Mohamed Amer
effatcartoon@hotmail.com

Message from & to Denmark FECO !!

This is a letter to Pharos Magazine

Effat, my dear friend,

I se that you express a lot of hatred towards my country and my flag. What have i done to offend you?

Peter Omann "omann@post4.tele.dk"

Danish FECO member

This is a letter answer to Mr. Peter Omann

Dear friend Peter Omann

Thank you for your kindly mail, firstly, I would like to tell you that you don't offend me at all, but are you agree about the cartoons which drawing by your Danish cartoonists ?!! and I would like to inform you that No contempt and abuse for the religions & prophets at all are you understand what I mean my friend ? thank you again for your e-mail, and there no any thing between me and you and I respect you,

I look to hear from you soon, with my best wishes. Sincerely,

Ismail, M. EFFAT

President FECO Egypt

This is a letter answer from Mr. Peter Omann

Thank you for your kind reply, my dear Effat. I am doing my very best to understand your reactions - and of course: I would be offended if you offended someone I love - (as I beleive you love your Prophet). But why make pictures of my flag whith snakes in the holy white cross - and why on earth put the star of Israel on my flag? Still: I insist to understand you and your feelings. (My wife and I even thought of going to Egybt to talk and learn - to help solve this crisis in a peaceful manner. But it's supposed to be too dangerous for Danes to visit your country these days. What a pity.)

Sincerely

Peter Omann

Hany Mohamed Mohamed El-Sagher
effatcartoon@hotmail.com

Mohamed Mousbah Shaaban
effatcartoon@hotmail.com

Dear EFFAT

I'm so glad after getting Ur Pharaohs issue 35.Gramercy to U sir. There is some problem regarding downloading the issue.I found some of the pages showing damaged.My poor fate....! I'm a cartoonist from Bangladesh ,presently working in a national daily the AMAR DESH.I achieved the only cartoonist award "Unmad Cartoonist Padak-2005"incepted by the renowned cartoon and satire magazine Unmad for the first time in Bangladesh. I'll feel proud if i my works publish in ur PHARAOHS. best regards.

Ahmed Kabir Kishore

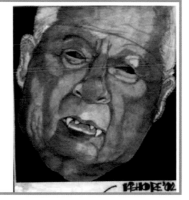

3. The Iranian response: the Jews must pay!

In February 2006 *Hamshahri*, Iran's largest circulation newspaper, announced a competition for cartoons about the Holocaust in response to the publication of caricatures of the Prophet Muhammad in European papers. The first obvious question is why choose the Shoah to respond to a series of cartoons published in a Christian country and/or to test the limits of freedom of expression? The Danish cartoon affair has nothing whatsoever to do with Israel, the Jewish people, let alone the Holocaust. Wouldn't it be more logical to test the limits of freedom of expression by mocking the Danish Royal family for example, or Christianity as such? There are endless possibilities, from Jesus to the Pope!

Perhaps, if one doesn't take into consideration the depth of today hatred towards the Jews in the Middle East! Obviously, the Shoah was not chosen by chance. It followed a series of anti-Israeli outbursts from Ahmadinejad, including a call for the Jewish state to be wiped off the map.

The sad fact is that the Iranians leaders really believe that:

1. the Jews are the real Masters of the West, behind all the so-called 'Christian' attacks against Islam (cf. above and below).
2. the Shoah is a myth. The previous cartoons demonstrated that Holocaust denial has been widespread throughout the Arab-Muslim world for years.

Iran's fiercely anti-Israeli regime is supportive of so-called Holocaust denial historians, who maintain that the systematic slaughter by the Nazis of mainland Europe's Jews as well as other groups during the Second World War has been either invented or exaggerated. Iran's hardline President Mahmoud Ahmadinejad prompted international anger when he dismissed the Nazi attempt to exterminate Europe's Jews as a 'myth' used to justify the creation of Israel.

The Iranian foreign ministry also invited British Prime Minister Tony Blair to Tehran to take part in a planned conference on the Holocaust, even though the idea had been branded by Blair as 'shocking, ridiculous, stupid'. Blair also said Ahmadinejad 'should come and see the evidence of the Holocaust for himself in the countries of Europe', to which Iran responded by saying it was willing to send a team of 'independent investigators'.

The next images are chosen from the 750 cartoons submitted from all over the world. More than 200 images on public display in an exhibition at Tehran's Palestine Contemporary Art Museum. The exhibition's opening was attended by the de facto Palestinian ambassador to Iran, Salah al-Zawawi, who has full diplomatic status in Tehran.

The exhibition's central theme is a contention that the death toll of the Shoah is exaggerated, and compares the Nazis' behaviour to Israel's treatment of the Palestinians. *'We are concerned about the real holocaust, which is happening to Palestinians,'* said Massoud Shojai Tabatabai, director of the Iranian House of Cartoons which co-ordinated the project. *'Why should Palestinians pay for events which happened thousands of kilometres away in Europe?'*

The organisers of the competition are 'honest Holocaust deniers' as one can see in the e-mail we received from M. Massoud Shojai Tabatabai, also director of Iran's cartoon website.

Dear Dr. Joel Kotek
Hi
Happy eid-el-fatir
Thanks a lot for your kindly attention. You could use all the cartoons for publishing or etc. It is free to clear up , what is the real holocaust. We have 3 reasonable questions:
1) Why discussion is not allowed concerning holocaust, if it is a
   historical fact.

2) The holocaust had been finished and nothing can be done for it. But the bigger holocausts are happening in Iraq, Palestine and Afghanistan and we can protect their victims.

3) Why suppressed and suffered people of Palestine living hundreds kilometres away from Poland and Germany should pay the price for holocaust?

Please keep in touch

Best wishes

Massoud Shojai

Let's hope that the honorable M. Shojai will soon acknowledge that the Jews have been a part of the Middle East for more than 3,000 years. In fact, the Iranian Jewish community is one of the oldest in the world, being descended from Jews who remained in the region following the Babylonian captivity. They settled in Iran at least a thousand years before the adoption of Islam by the Persian people. Let's hope too that he will discover Persia… Zionist past. The Torah tells how in 565 BCE Cyrus the Great granted the Judeans, exiled in Babylon, permission to return to Jerusalem and authorised them to rebuild the Temple destroyed during the siege of Nebuchadnezzar.

Some examples of cartoons presented to the competition

As our readers will see, through some examples, these cartoons do not promote freedom of speech. Rather they illustrate racist hatred and incitement to violence against the Jews.

Morocco

Abdellah Derkaoui

Morocco

Naji Benaji
Special Prize: 3 Gold Coins + Trophy +Honourable Mention

Turkey – Syria

Sadik Pala (Turkey)

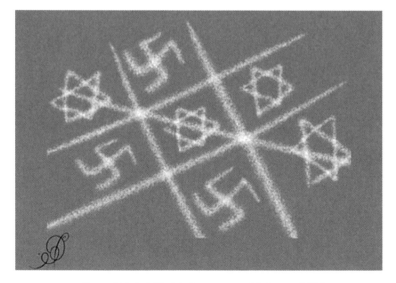

Youssef Mohaf (Syria), *Irancartoon*, 16 August 2006

Indonesia

Tommy Thomdean

Tommy Thomdean

Jordan

Jihad Awrtani

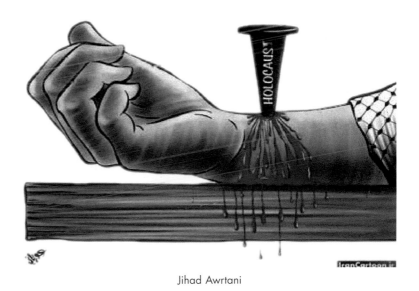

Jihad Awrtani

Iran

Amir Vahedi

Abdolhossein Amirizadeh

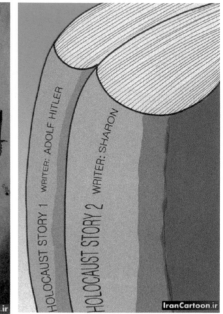

Soheil Setayesh

Maassoume Hamzelou Safai

Hadi Tabasi, *Irancartoon.ir*, 8 May 2006

Bernard Kurt Vennekohl (USA)

Sidney Marques (Brazil)

Benjamin Heine (Belgium)

Raul Erkinbaev (Russia)

Stefan Penev (Bulgaria)

The result of the competition: antisemitism as usual!

Chard/France
Second Prize: $4000 + Trophy + Honourable Mention

Derkaoui Abdellah/Morrocco
First Prize: $12000 + trophy + Honourable Mention

Carlos Latuff/Brazil
Second Prize: $4000 + trophy + Honourable Mention

One of the tied second prizes went to Françoise Pichard, alias Chard, who regularly draws cartoons for the daily *Présent* and the weekly *Rivarol*, two extreme-right publications connected to the Jean-Marie Le Pen's National Front. *Rivarol*'s director is expected to stand trial for running an interview in which extreme-right leader Le Pen denied the brutality of Nazi rule. France has very strict laws against denying the Holocaust. The strange fact is that the cartoon drawn by Chard did not appear on the official contest website. It certainly proves the political character of the results: Chard is an acknowledged denier of the Holocaust, and supporter of Robert Faurisson.

When extremes meet!

The results of the competition were shameful but logical: the cartoons cover all aspects of traditional and modern European antisemitism, from Satanism to deicide and Holocaust denial. How can we forget that 65 years ago, such images made the route to Auschwitz entirely acceptable?

Appendix 4

Arab Cartoonists' Response To Gaza Violence: Holocaust Analogies And Anti-Semitism

(Posted by the ADL: March 13, 2008 - www.adl.org/PresRele/ASaw_14/5245_14.htm)

New York, NY, March 3, 2008 … The barrage of rocket fire from Gaza and Israel's military action to stem the attacks on its cities have prompted an outpouring of "deeply offensive and bigoted" commentary in the Arab press, whose response has come in the form of a series of rapid-fire editorial cartoons using swastikas, classical anti-Semitic images and other hateful references to the Holocaust to vilify Israel and portray the Jewish state as an aggressor with genocidal ambitions.

The Anti-Defamation League (ADL) has posted online a selection of the most recent editorial cartoons, including cartoons appearing in Egyptian, Jordanian, and Palestinian newspapers.

"While it is not surprising that the editorial cartoonists would focus their criticism on Israel, their doing so with a mix of deeply offensive and bigoted Holocaust imagery, Jewish religious symbolism and vile stereotypes is breathtaking and at times quite shocking," said Abraham H. Foxman ADL National Director. "While we do not expect the Arab media to have a balanced view of the situation, the level of animosity and hate being aimed against Israel and Jews in response to the situation in Gaza is staggering."

One Jordanian cartoonist, in an image labeled "Gaza's Holocaust," (Al-Ghad, March 3) drew an Israeli attack helicopter shaped like a menorah blazing with gunfire and with its rotor blades shaped into the form of a swastika.

Other cartoons use similar Holocaust analogies and themes, with the Nazi swastika appearing in many of the images. Israelis and Jews are portrayed as child killers and brutal assassins, while no mention is made of the Palestinian terrorists responsible for the rockets that have injured and killed scores of Israeli civilians, or the role Hamas has played in promoting the attacks.

"We have always said that it is OK to criticize Israel. But these images clearly cross the line," said Mr. Foxman. "Not only do they outrageously equate Israel's military response to rocket attacks to the Holocaust, but draw upon classic stereotypical representations of Jews that were used as a tool by the Nazis themselves to incite anti-Semitism."

Holocaust imagery and direct comparisons to the Holocaust are a common feature of the anti-Semitic cartoons that regularly appear in Arab newspapers across the Middle East and throughout the Muslim world

Al-Ahram weekly, March 6-12, 2008 (Egypt)

Al-Ahram weekly, March 6-12, 2008 (Egypt)

Ad-Dustur, March 5, 2008 (Jordan)
In Arabic: "the only democracy in the Middle East."

Al-Jazira, March 5, 2008
In Arabic: "Olmert."

Al-Watan, March 4, 2008 (Qatar)

Ad-Dustur, March 4, 2008 (Jordan)
Israeli soldiers raise the Nazi flag over the dead bodies of the
Palestinians in "Gaza;" the cartoon mimics the famous photo of
U.S. Marines raising the flag at the battle of Iwo Jima.

Al-Khabar, March 4, 2008 (Algeria)
The cartoon's headline reads: «The New Nazism». Israeli Prime
Minister Ehud Olmert is depicted as Adolf Hitler.

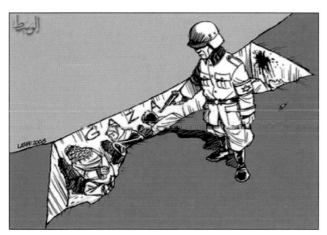

Al-Wasat, March 4, 2008 (Egypt)

Al-Ghad, March 3, 2008 (Jordan)
The cartoon's headline: "Gaza's Holocaust."

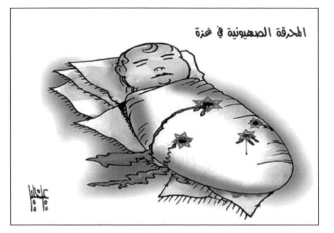

المحرقة الصهيونية في غزة

Al-Khalij, March 2, 2008 (UAE)
The cartoon's headline: "The Zionist Holocaust in Gaza."

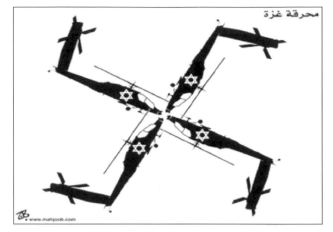

محرقة غزة

Al-Quds al-'Arabi, March 3, 2008 (UK)
The cartoon's headline: "Gaza's Holocaust."

هولوكوست إسرائيلية على غزة..

Filastin, March 3, 2008 (PA)
The cartoon's headline: "Israeli Holocaust in Gaza."

الشرعية الدولية

Al-Gumhuriyya, March 3, 2008 (Egypt)
The caption above reads: "The International Legitimacy." On the paper, in Arabic: "Gaza's Holocaust."

Main Arab daily and weekly newspapers

- *Ad Dustour* (*The Constitution*), Jordan, since 1967, daily, circulation 600,000
- *Al Goumhouriya* (*The Republic*), Egypt, since 1953, daily, circulation 1,500,000
- *Al Hayat* (*The Life*), London/Saudi Arabia, daily, circulation 110,000
- *Al Hayat al-Jadida* (*New Life*), Ramallah (Palestinian National Authority), Palestine, daily, circulation 6,000
- *Akhbar Al Khaleej* (*The News from the Gulf*), Bahrain, since 1976, daily, 1976, circulation 32,000
- *Al Khaleej* (*The Gulf*), UAE, since 1970, daily, circulation 75,000
- *Akhbar Al Yom* (The Daily News), Egypt, since 1944, daily
- *Al Ahram* (*The Pyramids*), Egypt, since 1875, daily, circulation 900,000
- *Al Ahram weekly*, Egypt, since 1991, weekly, English, circulation 60,000
- *Al Ayyam* (*The Days*), Palestine, since 1995, daily, circulation 10,000
- *Al Quds Al Arabi* (*The Arab Jerusalem*), pan-Arab (London), since 1978, circulation 50,000
- *Al Ittihad,* United Arab Emirates, daily
- *Al Ra'I* (*Opinion*), Jordan, daily, circulation 20,000
- *Al Sharq* (*The Orient*), Qatar, since 1985, daily, circulation 47,000
- *Al Raya* (*The Flag*), Qatar, since 1979, daily, circulation 18,000
- *Al Riyadh*, Saudi Arabia, since 1965, circulation 150,000
- *Al Watan* (*The Homeland*), Oman, since 1971, daily, circulation 34,000
- *Al Watan*, Qatar, since 1995, daily, circulation 15,000
- *Al Watan*, Kuwait, since 1974, daily, circulation 86,000
- *Al Watan*, Saudi Arabia, since 2000, daily, circulation 150,000
- *Asharq al-Awsat* (*The Middle East*), London/Saudi Arabia, since 1978, daily, circulation 235,000
- *Daily Star*, Lebanon, daily, circulation 15,000
- *Rose el-Youssef*, Egypt, weekly, circulation 120,000
- *Teshreen* (*October*), Syria, daily, circulation 50,000

Notes

Introduction

[1] Theodor Lessing, *La Haine de soi: le refus d'être juif*, translated from German and presented by Maurice-Ruben Hayoun (Paris: Berg International, 1990; new edn 2001). Lessing was one of the first victims of National Socialism, as Czech President Masaryk emphasised at his funeral.

[2] To clarify: a Jew may be considered an antisemite, for instance, if he hates his own identity and racist when this hatred is displayed towards someone other than a Jew.

[3] Bernard Lewis, 'Islam: What Went Wrong?', *Atlantic Monthly* (January 2002).

[4] Christian Delporte, *Les Crayons de la propagande, dessinateurs et dessin politique sous l'occupation* (Paris: CNRS éditions, 1993), pp.6–7.

[5] Ouriel Reshef, *Guerre, mythes et caricatures au berceau d'une mentalité française* (Paris: PFNSP, 1984), p.13.

[6] We have taken the concept of 'antisemyth' from Marie-Anne Matard-Bonucci, who employs it in an article that appeared in *XXᵉ siècle, revue d'histoire*, published by the Fondation nationale des Sciences Politiques de Paris, 'L'image, figure majeure du discours antisémite' (October–December 2001), pp.27–39. What is an 'antisemyth'? It is a charge, mostly of medieval origin, levelled solely against the Jews. The most familiar clichés are those of the Jew as deicide, killer of children, and finally of the vampire Jew.

[7] Matard-Bonucci, 'L'image, figure majeure du discours antisémite', pp.28–9.

Chapter 1

[8] See the reference work by Eduard Fuchs, *Die Juden in der Karikatur* (Munich: Albert Langen, 1921).

[9] See Gavin I. Langmuir, *History, Religion, and Antisemitism* (Berkeley and Los Angeles: University of California Press, 1993); *Toward a Definition of Antisemitism* (Berkeley and Los Angeles, 1996); Miri Rubin, *Gentile Tales: The Narrative Assault on Late Medieval Jews* (London and New Haven, CT: Yale University Press, 1999); Robert S. Wistrich, *Demonizing the Other: Antisemitism, Racism and Xenophobia* (Amsterdam: Harwood Academic, 1999; published with the Vidal *Sassoon International Centre for the Study of Antisemitism*, Hebrew University of Jerusalem).

[10] Léon Poliakov notes that charges of murder committed for magical or evil purposes can be found in every country and in all latitudes. In fourteenth-century China, Christian missionaries were accused of stealing children and ripping out their heart or eyes to produce charms or remedies. In Indochina the local population attributed this type of crime to the Chettys sect. In Madagascar at the time of Gallieni, the same charge was levelled against the agents of the French government. In antiquity the Jews were similarly accused by the Greeks, the first Christians by the Romans, and Gnostics, stylites and members of other sects by the Christians. It is a virtually universal theme, a veritable archetype that surfaces whenever alarming and hated foreigners threaten a society. Léon Poliakov, *Histoire de l'antisémitisme*. Vol.1. *L'Âge de la foi* (Paris: Éditions du Seuil, 1981), coll. 'Points-histoire', p.254.

[11] Deborah Jo Miller, Cornell University, rightly points out that it is wrong to confuse two myths of different origins, that are frequently linked. Cf. 'The Development of the "Ritual Murder" Accusation in the Twelfth and Thirteenth Centuries and its Relationship to the Changing Attitudes of Christians towards Jews', M. Phil. thesis, Cambridge University, 1991.

[12] Jean Delumeau, *La peur en occident (XIVᵉ-XVIIIᵉ siècle): une cité assiégée* (Paris: Fayard, 1978), see Chapter IX, esp. 'Le Juif, mal absolu', pp.273–304.

[13] Jules Michelet, *Le Moyen Age* (Paris: Robert Laffont, 1981), pp.481–2.

[14] Even in ancient Egypt, the author Damocrites maintained that every seven years the Jews had to take a stranger captive, bring him to their Temple and sacrifice him by cutting him in pieces. Apion of Alexandria, saying that the Jews fattened up a Greek, who was then sacrificed and eaten, took up this myth again.

[15] M.R. James, '*The Life and Miracles of St. William of Norwich*' by Thomas of Monmouth (Cambridge: Cambridge University Press, 1896).

[16] See Poliakov, *Histoire de l'antisémitisme*, 'Points-histoire', p.255; and Langmuir, *History, Religion, and Antisemitism*.

[17] The notion that the Jews killed Jesus has been the justification for centuries of anti-Jewish persecution. In the sixteenth century the Council of Trent attempted to remedy the problem by stating that '*the crime of the Crucifixion of Jesus is far more deeply rooted in us Christians than with the Jews… as we worship Him as the Lord and we deny Him by our actions and raise our hands in violence against him.*' The text goes on to say that Christ died '*at the moment that He Himself decided to die, and by internal consent*'. This four centuries-old text exonerating the Jews had no effect on the less enlightened masses, whose leaders perpetuated the accusation and fed the hatred of the Jews. Nevertheless, the charge of deicide continued to feature as an article of faith for many Christians right up to the time of Vatican Council II (1962–65).

[18] 'The Prioress's Tale', in Chaucer's Canterbury Tales, introduction and translation by Juliette Dor (Paris: Christian Bourgois, 1991), coll. 10/18, pp.192–6. In 1955 Anglican authorities dismantled the shrine at Lincoln cathedral and incised the confession that such 'fictions cost many innocent Jews their lives' (http://www.hcacentre.org/BloodLibel.html – Centre for the Study of Historical Christian Antisemitism).

[19] See Anna Esposito, 'The Ritual Murder Stereotype in the Trials of Trent and the Cult of the "Beatus" Simone', in Susanna Buttaroni and Stanisław Musiał, *Ritual Murder Legend in European History*, book and CDrom produced by the Association for Cultural Initiatives, Krakow, 2003.

[20] Another case of sanctification is worth mentioning: little André of Rinn (Austria), allegedly murdered by the Jews in 1462 and beatified in 1752.

[21] Jean des Preis (Liège, 1338–1400), known as Jean d'Outremeuse, was a clerk in Liège. He wrote a sort of universal prose history going back to the capture of Troy up to 1340. *Li Myreur des histors* (*The Historical Mirror*) is a work containing all manner of legends mingled with true stories, as well as passages from ancient texts rewritten in prose, such as *Ogier le Danois* or *La Geste de Liège*. See also Yves Chevalier, *L'Antisémitisme* (Paris: Cerf, 1984).

[22] In 1948 research conducted at the Weizmann Institute of Science, Rehovot, Israel, demonstrated that flour used for the Host is liable to attack by a blood-red fungus, *bacterium prodigiosum*. In 1969 Drs Yves Frey, Irène Georgantis and Odile Morisseau at the Blois Institute of Pharmacology reached the same conclusion.

[23] Co-religionists in Louvain met a similar fate. Salomon Ullmann, *Histoire des Juifs*

en Belgique jusqu'au XVIIIe siècle, notes et documents (Anvers: Delplace, 1927), p.21. See also Georges-Henri Dumont, Histoire de Bruxelles, biographie d'une capitale (Bruxelles: Le Cri, 1999). Further, the work of Didier Pasamonik, in particular his article 'Hosties sanglantes aux origines de la bande dessinée belge' ('Bleeding Hosts featuring in Belgian strip cartoons origin'), in La Diaspora des Bulles, to be published by Denoël, Paris, in 2007.

24 'The Sacrament of the Miracle has played an important role as the national symbol, marking the Catholic identity of the land', states a leaflet distributed to visitors to the Cathedral where the kings of the Belgians are consecrated. An outlined insert in the same document points out that 'The cult of the relic forms part of the struggle against the Jews, Protestants and free-thinkers. Charles V and the Habsburgs presented the stained glass windows. The Belgian kings Leopold I and Leopold II presented the first windows in the aisles. The country's noble families presented others. After 1870 the relic lost its national significance. But local devotion to the Sacrament of the Miracle continued up to the time of the Second World War. The windows, paintings and tapestries perpetuated the narrative of the alleged profanation of the Hosts by the Jews. It was not until after the Holocaust and under modern influence that a more critical attitude towards this medieval anti-Jewish legend was adopted in Catholic circles... In 1968, having taken into consideration the historical research into the subject, in the spirit of the Second Vatican Council the diocesan authorities of the archbishopric of Malines-Bruxelles acknowledged the tendentious nature of the accusation and the legendary presentation of the miracle.' See also Pasamonik, 'Hosties sanglantes aux origines de la bande dessinée belge'.

25 Quoted by Ladan Niayesh, Une Spécialité anglaise: le juif cannibale (An English Speciality: The Cannibal Jew) (Université de Montpellier III, CERRA).

26 Langmuir, History, Religion, and Antisemitism; and Poliakov, Histoire de l'antisémitisme.

27 Ibid.; and Joshua Trachtenberg, The Devil and the Jews (Philadelphia: JPS, 1983).

28 This edifying explanation appears in an article published in June 1943 by a certain Jacques Savary in Le Téméraire, the only magazine for youngsters published in Paris during the Nazi Occupation, at the time when the Jews were being hunted down and rounded up. See Pascal Ory, Le Petit Nazi illustré, vie et survie du 'Téméraire' (1943–44), preface by Léon Poliakov (Paris: Nautilus, 2002), p.69.

29 Daniel Tollet (dir.), Les Textes judéophobes et judéophiles dans l'Europe chrétienne et l'époque moderne (Paris: Presses Universitaires de France, 2000), coll. 'Histoires'.

30 Leviticus XVII, 10, J.H. Hertz edition of Pentateuch and Haftorahs, published by Soncino Press.

31 See Brigitte Sion, op. cit.

32 Pierre Chaunu, in Tollet, Les Textes judéophobes, p.viii.

33 Krzysztof Link-Lenczowski, 'Les textes judéophiles et judéophobes en Pologne aux XVIIe et XVIIIe siècles', in Tollet, Les Textes judéophobes, pp.205–16.

34 Jacek Wijaczka, 'Accusations and Legal Proceedings of Ritual Murder in the Republic of Poland-Lithuania during the 16th and 17th Centuries', in Buttaroni and Musiał, Ritual Murder Legend in European History.

35 See the Hagalil website, www.hagalil.com/czech/juedische-geschichte/hilsner/hilsner.

36 Guy Jucquois and Pierre Sauvage, L'Invention de l'antisémitisme racial, l'implication des catholiques français et belges (1850-2000) (Louvain-la-Neuve:Academia Bruylant, 2001), p.122.

37 Ibid.

38 Pierre Sorlin, 'La Croix' et les Juifs (1880-1899), contribution à l'histoire de l'antisémitisme (Grasset, 1967), pp.142–3.

40 Quoted by ibid., p.140.

41 Matard-Bonucci, 'L'image, figure majeure du discours antisémite', p.32.

42 Randall Bytwerk, Julius Streicher: The Man Who Persuaded a Nation to Hate Jews (New York: Stein & Day, 1983).

43 Raul Hilberg, The Destruction of the European Jew, 3 vols. (New Haven and London: Yale University Press, 2003). Most of the cartoons below come from the US Holocaust Museum in Washington.

Chapter 2

44 The protection was only relative, maintains F. Lovsky: the murder of a Jew (or a Christian) was indeed punishable, but not by the death penalty. See Fadiedy Lovsky, Antisémitisme et mystère d'Israël (Paris: Albin Michel, 1955), p.245.

45 Bernard Lewis, Sémites and anti-sémites (Paris: Presse pocket, 1986), coll. 'Agora', 83, p.154.

46 See ibid., p.150.

47 Ronald L. Nettler, 'Islamic Archetypes of the Jews: Then and Now', in Robert S Wistrich (ed.), Anti-Zionism and Anti-Semitism in the Contemporary World (New York: New York University Press, 1990), pp.78–83.

48 See Lovsky, Antisémitisme et mystère d'Israël, p.246. Blue was for Christians.

49 Lewis, Sémites and anti-sémites, p.167–8.

50 Jonathan Frankel, The Damascus Affair: 'Ritual Murder', Politics, and the Jews in 1840 (Cambridge: Cambridge University Press, 1997).

51 Ibid., p.250.

52 See the ADL website. These two images came from an Israeli television programme on the subject.

53 Article headed: 'A special ingredient used during the festival of Purim, was the blood of gentile adolescents'.

54 The title, 'Just water, only water', as well as the contents of this letter refer to the Wazzani, tributary of the Hasbani River, which the Lebanese at the command of Syria decided to divert on 16 October, the day before the French summit. Israel refused to permit the diversion of this precious asset (that flows into Lake Tiberias).

55 See the website palestinefacts.org/pf_1991to_now_davos_2001.php.

56 Founder of several satirical papers (La Caricature, Charivari and Le Journal amusant), Charles Philipon is the father of French cartoons. He was imprisoned in 1834. His paper La Caricature was banned in 1834. See Martine Contensou, Balzac et Philipon Associés - Grands Fabricants de Caricatures en Tous Genres (Paris: Paris-Musées, 1991); as well as J. Valmy-Baysse, André Gil, L'Impertinent (Paris: éditions du Félin, 1991). See also Annie Duprat and Pascal Dupuy, in Cahiers d'Histoire, special issue dedicated to the art of the cartoon, 'La Caricature entre subversion et réaction', no.75 (Spring 1999), Introduction.

57 Interview with Michel Kischka by Joël Kotek, New York, 2 February 2002.

58-59 This is the case particularly in Lebanon and strangely enough in Algeria. Dilem, for instance, is the best example of an intelligent and courageous Algerian cartoonist. It is by no coincidence that he is more than often threatened with jail. That's why his gifted colleague Slim is in exile in Paris. Dilem and Slim are the antithesis of all the other Arab cartoonists. Their cartoons are first and foremost aimed at Algerian politics.

60 Michaël Prazan and Tristan Mendès-France, 'Parcours d'une haine antisémite', Durban2001.com.

61 See 'Speak frankly...', an interview with Baha Bukhari, one of the best Palestinian

199

cartoonists, by Alessandra Antonelli, *Palestine Report*, vol.5, no.12, 4 September 1998: 'Yes, many people think that he has been assassinated by the OLP.'

[62] Ben Lynfield, 'Palestinian's keen caricatures keep censors occupied', *Christian Science Monitor*, 28 November 2001.

[63] Atatürk would have been a *dönme*, a secret Jew who would have overthrown the Ottoman sultans to punish them for refusing to hand Palestine to the Zionists. Although completely unfounded this allegation is widespread in integrationist literature. See Lewis, *Sémites and anti-sémites*, p.249.

[64] These three cartoons are taken from Ohad Zmora (ed.), *Israël doit être détruit, recueil de caricatures de la presse arabe* (Tel Aviv: Tsahal information office, July 1967). Michël Prazan et Tristan Mendès-France, 'Survey of antisemitic hatred', *Durban 2001.com* and the ProChoix review (Paris).

[65] Raphaël Israeli, *Une image démoniaque du Juif* (Paris: L'Arche, September 2001), p.92.

Chapter 4

[66] www.intifada.com/frachildhood.

[67] See Israel-state-terrorism.org.

[68] *Al-Hayat Al-Jadida,* 24 December 2001, broadcast (PMW).

[69] The Independent Media Centre is an international information network created on the occasion of the mobilisation of Seattle. It exists in some thirty countries. Contrary to all professional practice *Indymedia* does not take the trouble to verify information. This 'independent' agency, fuelled by its militancy, makes do with the anti-Israeli argument.

[70] belgium.indymedia.org/front.php3?article_id=15904&group=webcast.

[70] Press release from the Palestinian Committee on the Rights of Man, 3 March, 2002.

[71] See John Podhoretz, 'Hatefest by the bay', *New York Post*, 14 May 2002.

[73] Plantu is the most famous French cartoonist. He publishes daily in *Le Monde*. Konk used to draw for *Le Monde* too but was fired since he supported Faurisson, the notorious French Holocaust denier.

[74] *Le Monde*, 7 August 2002.

[75] As a longstanding admirer of his work, I first met Willem almost 20 years ago in Oxford, at the first World Conference on the Holocaust, organised by the late Robert Maxwell. The encounter was fascinating. It made us realise that it is possible inadvertently to employ antisemitic graphic vocabulary without in any way having antisemitic provocative intentions. Willem is definitively a great and pure artist.

[76] *Libération*, 29 December 2002.

[77] The first caricature and cartoon web contest (www.irancartoon.com/cartooncontest/index).

[79] The great French daily is actually excused by the intervention of Robert Solé, referring to this 'absurd comparison made by a Kenyan newspaper'.

[80] Wladimir Jankelevitch, *L'Imprescriptible: pardonner dans l'honneur et la dignité?* (Paris: Seuil, 1996), p.88.

[81] Alain Finkielkraut, 'Une croix gammée à la place de l'étoile', *l'Arche*, May–June 2002.

[82] All those cartoons have been collected by Leon Saltiel. They are also partly reproduced by the ADL (see 'Calls On Greek Government To Condemn Anti-Semitism In The Press', 22 July 2002).

[83] Michel Taubmann, Florence Taubmann, Pierre-André Taguieff, Pascal Perrineau, Gérard Grunberg, Illios Yannakakis, 'Contre l'antisionisme, pour la paix, faute d'une critique politique du gouvernement Sharon, beaucoup d'intellectuels s'atta-

quent à l'existence même d'Israël', *Le Figaro*, 23 March 2002.

[84] Pierre-André Taguieff, *La Nouvelle Judéophobie* (Paris: Les Mille et une Nuits, 2002).

[85] These cartoons appear mostly on 'anti-globalisation' sites, some of which are sections of *Indymedia*. They can be found on the Gush Shalom site, the ultra-leftist Israeli movement, on the Centre d'Etudes Internationales de l'Université de Liège (CAPRI) and even on *Holywar.org*, agency of the most radical Catholic far right.

[86] www.indymedia.org/front.php3?article_id=122288&group=webcast;;france.indymedia.org ; www.antiglobalizacion.org/

[87] See also Stéphane Foucart and Stéphane Mandard, 'Le réseau *Indymedia* en proie à des dérives antisémites', *Le Monde*, 9 July 2002.

Chapter 5

[88] Thoughts on Durban, see www.ptb.be/international/article.phtml?section, 6 September 2001.

[89] See *Plus magazine*, 168, January 2002, p.29.

[90] It was at the feet of the Latin patriarch that Galand went to confirm his ideological convictions during his mission to Palestine in November and December 2001. See OXFAM-Info, no.123, Autumn 2001.

[91] Taguieff, *La nouvelle judéophobie*, p.192.

[92] Interview broadcast on 10 October 2000 at l p.m on French language news on Belgian radio. It should be stressed that the ex-director Oxfam Belgium and President of the Belgian-Palestine Friends did not wait for the second intifada to declare his opposition to the Oslo accords and to call for an economic, scientific and cultural boycott of Israel. Back in 1997 he had already called for a boycott of Israel in the newspaper *Le Soir*: 'The European Union should decide to exert strong pressure on Israel … on their goods, their products, and economic, cultural and scientific agreements should be frozen … And it is advisable when the time comes for France and Belgium not to ratify the Europe-Israel partnership agreement'.

[93] David Nirenberg, 'Plus que les Juifs: le roi', *L'Histoire*, no.263 (October 2002), p.43.

[94] The princes made use of the Jews, in exchange for which the latter were supposed to receive protection, and benefit from various advantages and privileges. In actual fact the position of the Jewish communities ended up by being even more precarious, at the mercy of the demands and the whims of the powerful, who had no compunction in expelling them whenever they felt like it, and seizing their goods or making them the scapegoats for popular discontent.

[95] In France there were anti-Jewish outbursts every forty to fifty years after the Jews' emancipation. The socialism that emerged after the 1848 revolution was accompanied by violent ideological attacks on the Jews. Charles Fourier and Alphonse Toussenel were two extreme examples. The latter's *The Jews, Kings of the Epoch* appeared in 1844. In 1886, Edouard Drumont's book *Jewish France* launched a major antisemitic struggle, with the 1894 Dreyfus Affair as the apex.

[96] Foulek Ringelheim, *Edmond Picard, juriconsulte de Race* (Brussels: Larcier, 1998), p.64.

[97] Michel Winock, 'Emancipation et exclusion: La France et la question juive', *L'Histoire* (October 2002), p.53.

[98] Henri Arvon, *Les Juifs et l'idéologie* (Paris: Presses Universitaires de France, 1978), p.52. See also Joseph Gabel, *Réflexions sur l'avenir des Juifs* (Paris: Klincksieck, 1987), coll. 'Méridiens', p.67.

[99] Manuel Abramowicz, 'Demain des bombes?', *Regards,* no.490, 30 January–6 February 2001.

[99 bis] Caricature from *Sound Money*, August 1896, in Louise A. Mayo, *The Ambivalent Image: Nineteenth-Century America's Perception of the Jew* (London: Associated University Press, 1988).

[100] Malcolm Ross, *The Real Holocaust: The Attack on unborn children and life itself* (Stronghold, 1983). See Poppy Dixon, 'Blood Libel: The Roots of Racism and the Fear of Sex in the Pro-life Movement', postfun.com/pfp/features/98/oct/bloodlibel.

[101] www.islam-belgique.com/boycott2.cfm.

[102] Katy Bisraor, 'Ariel', the detergent with the same name as the Prime Minister of Israel, boycotted by the Egyptians and the Palestinians', *Proche-Orient info,* 4 December, 2002.

[103] See especially the news item on TF1 (French TV), 8 April, 2001.

[104] Ibid.

[105] Ibid.

[106] Albawaba.com.

[107] According to the site of the 2005 Iranian Short Film Festival (http://www.shortfilmfest-ir.com/2005/jury/jury_spritual_2005_page-3.htm), Hasan Bulkhari (b.1962) holds a Ph.D. in Islamic Philosophy and, among other things, teaches philosophy of art at Tabatabaei and Al-Zahra Universities in Iran and is a prolific author of literary and scientific works. According to the site, he is also counsellor and member of the Film Council of the Islamic Republic of Iran Broadcasting (IRIB) and a member of the IRIB's Approval Group - TV Films and Serials. An excerpt of the video was translated by the Middle East Media Research Institute. http://www.memritv.org/Transcript.asp?P1=1049.

[108] While it is difficult to attribute bias to Disney himself, the notion that he harboured antisemitism seems to have found some dark appeal. The truth is that he was a fierce conservative and anti-communist. Hating Disney has become a cliché.

[109] See René Girard and especially, *La Violence et le sacré* (Paris: Hachette Littérature, 2002), coll. 'Pluriel. Philosophie' (first edn 1972).

[110] Like it or not, Judaism remains the original matrix both for Christianity and for Islam, without which the latter could not make sense; hence all the ambiguity in relations with the Jews, at once the people of God and traitors to his message.

[111] Both Russia and China are untouchable. Permit me to quote here the 'cynical-realist' comment of a specialist on the Africa of the Great Lakes, Gerard Prunier, to the commission of enquiry of the Belgian Senate relating to the decision of the Hutu to exterminate the Tutsi. He regarded this decision as 'clumsy'. 'To imagine killing three quarters of a million human beings, and retain power afterwards is only possible if you are emperor of China, because one then has the capacity to sign huge contracts with Airbus or other companies, but when it is a matter of a little country like Rwanda, one is obliged to be relatively moral, because there are no huge contracts to sign. You only overlook crimes if they bring in something. Rwanda had nothing to offer to make us forget its crimes. The people at the very centre around Habyarimana, who thought they could extricate themselves from this business, were hugely naive, they were certainly unaware of what they were doing and of the world context in which they were operating.' (Senate, Legislative Document no.1-611/7).

[112] Taguieff, *La Nouvelle Judéophobie*, p.150.

[113] We were inspired by what Galtung wrote that appeared on Danny Schechter's website www.mediachannel.org. See also Galtung, *Essays in Peace Research*, 5 vols (Copenhagen: C. Ejlers, 1975-1980).

[114] Alfred Grosser, Les Occidentaux: *les pays d'Europe et les États-Unis depuis la guerre* (Paris, Seuil, 1982), coll. 'Points. Histoire', no.61, p.7.